구한말 최초의 순국열사 이한응

송재용 편저

제이앤씨
Publishing Corporation

『殉國烈士李漢應先生遺史』에서

2

『殉國烈士李漢應先生遺史』에서

묘소

당시 주영공사관(런던)의 현재 모습

주영공사관 정경
(건물의 보존 상태는 비교적 양호하였다. 외형은 원형에 가깝게 유지하고
있었으나 내부는 개·보수의 흔적이 보였다.)

주영공사관 주소

── 서 문

한국 학술진흥재단 중점연구소 지원 연구과제(단국대학교 동양학연구
소, 총괄과제 '개화기 대외 민간문화교류 자료초' 중 제2세부과제 '개화기
구미인들과의 민간문화교류 자료초')를 수행하기 위해 2001년 영국에 가
자료조사를 하던 중 이한응 관련 자료를 영국 공문서보관소(PRO)에서
입수(MF)하게 되었다. 한국에 돌아와 자료를 검토해 본 결과 연구과제와
밀접한 관련이 있을 뿐 아니라, 이한응의 애국심과 순국 정신을 세상에
알릴 필요가 있다고 판단하여 국내에 소장된 자료들을 조사 입수하였다.
이 과정에서 순국열사 이한응 선생 추모회에서 발간한 『순국열사이한응
선생유사』와 친손자인 이민섭 동국대 명예교수에게 이한응 관련 자료도
입수하였다. 그리고 국내 답사(용인시 덕성리 묘지 및 당질 이상준 등의
전의 이씨 면담)와 2002년 · 2005년 영국에 다시 가 자료조사를 하였다.
특히 2005년에는 이한응이 런던에 체류했던 거주지(Earl's Court 지역)
를 직접 방문 조사하고 촬영까지 함으로써 관련 자료들을 한층 풍부하게
수집할 수 있었다.

이한응은 주영공사서리로 일본이 한국을 병합하려 하자, 1905년 5월
12일 영국 런던에서 유서를 남기고 자결한 순국 제1호의 인물이다. 그럼
에도 불구하고 이한응에 대한 본격적인 연구는 거의 전무할 뿐만 아니라,
일반인들은 이한응이 어떤 인물인지 대부분 알지 못한다. 그러므로 저자는

순국열사 이한응을 널리 알릴 필요가 있다고 생각하여 출판을 결심하였다.

본서는 개화기에 한국인으로서는 최초로 당시 서양세계의 맹주격이었던 영국(런던)에 장기간 체류하면서 서양을 직접 경험하고 영어를 구사하여 서양과의 외교를 펼쳤던 이한응에 대한 연구(생애와 외교활동과 의의를 중심으로)와 자료(주로 영국 공문서보관소 소장 자료)에 초점을 맞추었다. 자료는 국내에 알려진 자료들은 제외하고 국내에 없거나 알려지지 않은 자료, 특히 영국 공문서보관소 자료들을 중심으로 엮었다. 그것은 국내에 소장된 자료는 구해볼 수 있지만, 영국 공문서보관소에 있는 자료는 구해 보기가 쉽지 않기 때문이다. 뿐만 아니라 국내 소장된 자료는 그리 많지도 않을뿐더러 자료적 가치 측면에서도 영국 공문서보관소 자료보다 질량면에서 떨어진다. 그러므로 이 분야 연구자들에게 국내 자료보다는 영국 공문서보관소 자료를 제공하는 것이 더 낫다고 판단하였다. 그리고 자료제공에 있어 잘못된 부분이나 오류는 저자의 책임임을 밝힌다.

이한응은 개화기 한국인으로서는 최초로 당시 서양문명의 중추를 이루고 있던 영국의 수도 런던에 장기간 체류한 인물이다. 따라서 본서는 개화기 한국인의 서양 이해의 실상을 밝히는데도 대단히 유용한 자료와 연구가 될 것이다.

이 책이 발간되기 까지에는 연구과제에 참여했던 오인영·김구래·이현우 선생의 도움이 있었다. 이분들께 감사를 드린다.

끝으로 이한응 선생의 친손자인 이민섭 동국대 명예교수와 출판을 흔쾌히 허락해 준 제이앤씨 사장님과 관계자 여러분에게 이 자리를 빌어 감사의 말씀을 드린다.

2007년 1월

한남동 연구실에서 송재용

목 차

구한말 최초의
순국열사 이한응

1 머리말 _____

사람은 한번 태어나면 언젠가는 죽게 마련이다. 그런데 주어진 삶을 인간답게 살지 못하고, 불의(不義)와 패악(悖惡)한 행동을 서슴지 않는 인간들이 비일비재한 것이 현실이다. 특히 구한말 국가와 민족의 운명이 풍전등화의 위기에 처한 상황에서 사리사욕에 눈이 어두워 일본에 나라와 민족을 팔아먹는 행위까지 한 역적들이 있었으니 이들을 어찌 용서할 수 있겠는가? 이 같은 친일 매국노들이 있는 반면, 나라와 민족을 위해 자신의 몸을 희생한 애국선열들의 고귀한 순절 또한 많았다. 그 중에서도 이 역만리 영국 땅에서 주영공사 서리로서 기울어져가는 나라를 구하고자 고군분투하다 맨 처음 순국의 길을 택한 이한응(李漢應)을 주목할 필요가 있다.

이한응은 1905년 5월 12일 조국의 암울한 앞날을 예견하고 32살의 짧은 생을 머나먼 이국땅에서 마감한 구한말의 대표적인 순국열사이다. 그는 유럽에서는 거의 유일한 조선의 외교관으로서 쓰러져가는 나라를 일으키고자 영국 정부에 외교적 노력을 기울였다. 그러나 당시의 상황은 복잡한 국내 정치와 일본의 방해로 인해 해외 공사관과 본국 정부 사이에는 연락조차 여의치 않았다. 이러한 상황에서 일개 공사 서리로 역사의 큰 흐름을 바꾸기에는 한계가 있음을 통분하여 자결하였다.

여기서는 이한응이 남긴 공사관 일지와 영국공문서보관소(PRO)의 자료들을 중심으로 그의 생애, 그리고 외교활동과 그 의의에 대해 대략적으로 살펴보고자 한다. 공사관일지는 이한응이 영국에 머물던 시기에 영국 신문을 중심으로 극동에 관한 정보를 담고 있는 기사들을 취합하여 공식적으로 작성한 자료이다. 그러나 이 일지는 이한응이 해당 기사에 대한 견해를 대부분 언급하고 있지 않아 스크랩 정도로 판단된다. 따라서 적극적으로 영국정부와 대화를 시도하였던 영국공문서보관서 자료와 상보적으로 살펴보는 것이 그의 생애와 외교활동 등을 조망하는데 바람직할 것으로 사료된다.

2 생애 _____

구한말 순국열사 이한응(李漢應)의 관향(貫鄕)은 전의(全義)이며, 자(字)는 경천(敬天), 호(號)는 국은(菊隱)이다. 시조(始祖)는 고려 때 태사공(太師公)을 지낸 이도(李棹)요, 부(父)는 곤양(昆陽 : 지금의 경남 사천군) 군수를 지내고 병조판서로 추증된 경호(璟鎬)요, 모(母)는 벽진(碧珍) 이씨이다. 이한응의 생부(生父)는 경호의 둘째형 명호(命鎬)이다. 이한응은 명호의 둘째 아들로 경호에게 계자(系子)하였다. 전의 이씨 이한응 가문은 명문거족으로 경기도 용인군 이동면에서 선대부터 세거(世居)하였다.

이한응은 고종 11년 갑술년(1874) 9월 21일에 출생하였다. 이때는 정치·경제·문화 등의 서구의 풍조가 극동의 나라인 조선에까지 흘러 들어오던 시기였다.

이한응이 출생하기 8년 전, 천주교도 학살을 문책의 구실로 삼아 이양선인 프랑스 군함이 강화도까지 쳐들어와 소요를 일으켰던 병인양요(1866)가 있었고, 그가 출생한 지 2년 후 운양호 포격사건(1875)을 이유로 조선에 온 일본의 사절단과 담판을 거듭한 끝에 병자수호조약(1876)이 체결되었던 시기였던 것이다.

그런데 이 동안에도 국내정계는 임오군란(1882)과 갑신정변(1884)을 위시해 파란곡절이 중첩하였으며, 수구파와 개혁파 간의 알력 분쟁과 더불어 청국과 일본의 대립이 첨예화되었다. 또한 서구제국과의 외교통상도 진척되어 고종 19년 임오년(1882)에 한미조약을 위시해서 영국·프랑스·독일 등 여러 나라와 외교조약을 체결하는 등 많은 변화를 보였던 시기였다.

　이러한 복잡한 국내외 정세 속에서 태어난 이한응은 어려서부터 명석한 두뇌와 의연한 행동으로 많은 사람의 기대를 한 몸에 받으며 성장하였다. 그리하여 그는 5세부터 한문을 공부하기 시작하였는데, 그 성취도가 매우 빨라 15세 때에는 상당한 경지에 도달하였다고 한다.

　그러나 세계적으로 거센 제국주의 세력이 국내에 들어오고 있는 상황에서, 시골에서 고루하게 재래식 한문이나 공부하고 있다는 것은 그의 총명과 예지가 허락하지 않았다. 이한응은 16세(1889)에 상경(上京)해서 관립영어학교에 입학하였다. 그가 관립영어학교에 입학하게 된 동기는 국가의 장래를 우려하는 마음과 경륜을 펼쳐 보이려는 포부가 있었던 바, 이를 위해 외국어를 배우고 익혀 국가와 민족을 위하여 활동무대를 국외로 넓히려는 의도가 있었던 것으로 짐작된다.

　그리하여 남다른 노력의 결과, 2년간의 학기를 우수한 성적으로 마쳤으며, 졸업 후에도 이용후생의 기회가 도래하기를 기다리며 계속 학문에 매진하였다. 그리고 당시 출사(出仕)의 수단이었던 과거, 즉 사마방(司馬榜)에 시부(詩賦)로 응시하여 성균관 진사에 합격한 것은 그의 나이 21세 되던 때인 고종 31년 갑오년(1894)이었다.

　그런데 갑오년에 불행히도 가정적으로 환경의 변화를 초래하는 일이 발생했다. 즉, '동학농민봉기'가 전라북도 고부에서 전봉준(全奉準)과 김개남(金介男) 등을 중심으로 일어났던 것이다. 이들은 한때 여러 군읍을 점령하였는데, 이때 그의 부친이 호남우영관(湖南右領官)으로 관군을 인솔하고 동학군 토벌에 출전하였다가 전사하였다. 그리하여 이한응은 지성을 다해 예(禮)에 따라 장례를 치루는 한편, 예법에 따라 3년 상기(喪期)를 마치었다.

　탈상 후 이한응이 첫 직책[한성부주사(漢城府主事)]에 임명된 것은 고종 34년 정유년(1897) 24세 되던 때이다. 그런데 이 동안에도 조선을 놓고 청국·일본·러시아 등 강대국들의 분쟁 알력은 끊이지 않았고, 국내 정국의 변화 또한 계속되었다. 동학농민봉기를 구실로 조선에 출병하였던 청·일 양국은 청일 전쟁을 치르고 난 뒤, 시모노세키조약(下關條約)에 의하여 청국은 조선의 완전독립국임을 승인함과 동시에 조선에서 손을 뗀 것처럼 보였지만, 사실은 수구파와 은연중 접촉하면서 다시 손을 뻗칠 시기를 노리고 있었다. 한편, 일본은 전쟁에서 승리한 여세를 이용하여 조선의 독립을 보장한다는 허울 좋은 명목을 내어 걸고 실제로는 침략 정책의 수행을 기도하였다. 일본은 조정 안팎에 친일 세력을 심어 놓고 실권 장악을 위하여 온갖 만행을 저지르던 중, 고종 32년(乙未)에는 명성황후 시해사건까지 일으켜서 국민을 극도로 격앙시켰다.

한편, 이런 외중에 친러파를 통해 조정 관원을 조종하는 러시아의 암약으로 인해서 고종 황제가 일 년간이나 러시아공사관에 파천하여 있는 등 대내·대외 정세는 다람쥐 쳇바퀴 돌아가듯 하였다. 그러다가 고종 황제가 내외국인의 권고에 의하여 정유년에 경운궁(지금 덕수궁)으로 환어(還御)한 후, 국호를 고쳐 대한(大韓) 그리고 연호를 제정하여 광무(光武)로 선포하고, 모든 정령을 일신한 후에야 국민들은 비로소 약간의 안정감이나마 가지게 되었다. 그러나 조정에서는 여전히 친일·친러·수구·개혁파 등의 세력이 정권쟁탈전을 벌여왔고, 러시아·일본 등 강대국 세력들은 야욕의 눈초리로 국토와 이권을 노리고 있던 것이 이때의 실정이었다. 이 같은 시기에 한성부 주사라는 미관말직에 처음으로 출사한 이한응은, 직위에 연연하지 않고 공무를 집행하는 데 전력을 다하였다.

그 후 2년 뒤인 광무 3년(1899) 이한응은 모교인 관립영어학교의 교관으로 전출하게 되었다. 여기서도 그는 일찍이 갈고 닦은 실력을 능동적으

로 활용하여 세계적 활약을 꿈꾸는 신진 청년들의 교육에 주력하였는데,
그 과정에서 탁월한 실력과 더불어 고매한 인격과 덕행으로 상하 사람들
의 신망을 크게 받았다. 그리하여 광무 5년(1901) 신축 3월에는 주차영의
양국공관(駐箚英義兩國公舘) 3등참서관(三等參書官)에 임명되어 공사
민영돈(閔泳敦)과 함께 영국의 수도 런던으로 부임하게 되었다. 여기서
부터 이한응의 오랜 열망인 국제무대에서의 활약의 길이 열리게 되었다.
이한응은 전통 유학과 영어 등 신학문을 겸비하여 외교무대에서 활동할
수 있는 기반을 갖추고 있었던 것이다.

　고매한 인격과 활발한 외교로 그의 신망이 대내외에 널리 알려졌던 바,
광무7년(1903) 10월에는 6품 통훈대부에서 정3품 통정대부로 특별히 가
자(加資)되었다. 그 다음 해인 갑진년 광무 8년(1904)에는 주영공사 민영
돈이 귀국함과 동시에 공사 서리로서 영국의 수도인 런던에 주재하면서
복잡하고도 중요한 대영외교의 모든 책임을 혼자 맡게 되었다.
조선을 둘러싸고 일어나는 열강의 각축 속에서 전락하여 가는 조국의 국
제적 지위, 이것은 해외사절로 나가 있는 애국일념의 그로써는 잠시도 우
려하지 않을 수 없는 일이었다. 또한 그는 암담한 환경에서 조국이 뚫고
나갈 활로를 모색하면서 영국 및 여러 외국과의 외교적 활동에서 유리한
성과를 얻기 위해 부단한 노력을 계속하였다. 그리고 매일매일 접수되는
외신보도의 주요 내용을 일지(日誌)로 적는 한편, 이를 통해 성찰과 연구
를 거듭하였다. 그러므로 그의 손으로 기록한 공사관 일지의 대부분의 기
록이 조선을 둘러싸고 움직이던 일본·러시아·영국 등의 국제적 동향이
었다는 사실만으로도 가히 당시 이한응의 외교적 안목과 애국심을 짐작
할 수 있다.

　특히 주목할 것은 당시 서울의 관리들과는 달리, 이한응은 조선의 장래

가 위험하다는 것을 파악했다는 점과, 러일전쟁이 일어날 것을 예견하고 이 전쟁의 승리국이 조선을 지배할 것임을 통찰하고 이를 방지하기 위해 영국 정부에 한반도 중립화 방안을 제시했다는 점이다. 그것도 한국 정부 가 일본의 견제를 받는 상황에서 독자적인 외교활동을 통해 제시했던 것 으로 짐작된다. 그의 이러한 외교활동은 구한말 국권 상실기에 있어 첫 순국이라는 사실로써만이 아니라, 탁월한 국제정세관으로 한국 외교사에 독특한 발자취를 남겼다는 점에서도 높이 평가된다.

당시 일본은 조선에 대한 강점 야욕을 숨기지 않은 채 대외적으로 조선 을 고립시키고자 노력하였다. 그 중 하나가 영일 동맹조약의 개정이었다. 이것은 일본이 러-일 강화조약을 맺기에 앞서 영국과 "일본이 한국에서 의 정치·경제·군사상의 지도감독 및 보호 등 조치를 취할 권리를 영국 은 인정한다"는 조문을 주로 하여 개정한 것이었다.

이한응은 비분강개의 피눈물을 뿌려 가면서 본국 정부와 연락을 취하 는 한편, 영일동맹 조문의 부당성을 영국 정부에 항의하였다. 그러나 식민 지 점령의 야욕으로 혈안이 된 이들 제국주의 강대국에게 약소국인 우리 의 항의가 용인될 리 만무하였다. 이는 당시 식민지 야욕을 채우기에 급 급했던 영국이나 이해당사국인 일본도 마찬가지였다. 또한 그들 정부만이 아니라 영국의 일반국민들까지도 한국인은 주권을 상실한 국민으로 간주 해 일상의 접촉에 있어서도 교오경모(驕傲輕侮)하기 짝이 없었다.

그럼에도 불구하고 이한응은 이러한 굴욕을 참으면서 일본이 우리나라 를 보호국으로 만들 것을 염려하여 각국에 주재하던 우리나라 공사들에 게 전보를 청하여 한자리에 모여 나라의 앞날을 대비하고자 하였으나, 하 나도 응하는 사람이 없었고, 얼마 후 대부분 조선으로 돌아가고 이한응만 홀로 영국에서 온갖 노력을 다하였다.

그러나 나라를 위한 일편단심으로 일관하여 온 이한응이었지만, 나라가 망하는 데에는 더 이상 버티어 나갈 힘이 없었던 것이었다. 망국의 조짐을 예견하고 흐르는 눈물로 베개를 적셔가며 그 타개책을 심사숙고하여 본 것도 여러 날 밤, 그러나 국제적으로 이미 상실된 주권을 다시 찾을 길이 없음을 절감하였다. 더구나 이한응은 4월부터 괴한 2명에게 살해 위협을 받고 있었는데 이는 런던 주재 일본 공사의 지시로 짐작된다. 그래서 그는 영국 정부에 신변보호를 요청하는 편지를 보낸 적이 있었다. 이에 영국 외무성은 내무성에 이러한 사실을 통보한 바 있다. 그러나 영국 경찰에서 신변보호를 실제로 했는지는 확인할 수 없다. 마침내 이한응은 비장한 결심을 하게 된다. 그는 영국 외무성의 고위 관리들에게 면담을 신청한 상태였지만, 성과가 없을 것으로 판단하여 스스로 면담을 포기하고 자결을 택했던 것 같다. 일개 외교관으로서 망해가는 나라를 되살릴 방법과 힘이 없는 상황에서 굴욕적이고 노예적인 삶을 사는 것보다는 일본의 천인공노할 만행에 항거하기 위해 죽기로 작정하였다. 이처럼 그는 자신의 한 몸을 조국에 깨끗이 희생으로 바치겠다고 마음먹었던 것이다.

"오호라 나라의 주권이 없어지고, 사람의 평등을 잃으니 모든 교섭에 치욕이 망극할 따름이다. 진실로 피를 가진 사람이라면 어찌 참고 견디리오. 나라가 장차 무너지고, 온 민족이 남의 노예가 되리라. 구차스럽게 산다는 것은 욕됨만 더할 따름이다. 이 어찌 죽는 것보다 낫겠는가? 죽을 뜻을 매듭지으니 다시 할 말이 없노라."

(광무 9년(1905) 을사 5월 12일(음력 4월9일))

주영 공사서리 이한응은 숙식을 겸하고 있던 공사관에서 이같은 심회를 언급한 유서와 함께 생가의 큰형 한풍(漢豊)과 부인 진주(晋州) 강씨에게 보내는 유언장을 남겨 놓고 주영공사관 부근 이발소에서 이발을 한 후, 공사관으로 돌아와 조용히 앉아 독약 그릇을 들어 마셨다. 그의 유서를 보면 영국 은행에 예치한 월급 가운데 천여 원은 반드시 시체운반비로 쓰고, 식비 등 세세한 부분까지 언급한 후, 생가의 동생 한승의 아들을 양자로 삼아 줄 것과 부인에게 어린 딸을 잘 기르라는 등의 유언을 남겼다. 여기서 그의 성품의 일면을 엿볼 수 있다.(필자가 조사한 바에 의하면, 그의 죽음에 대해 국내의 황성신문을 비롯해 영국의 LONDON TIMES 등 2-3개 신문에 보도된 것을 확인하였다.)

나라를 위해 목숨을 바친다는 것은 결코 쉬운 일이 아니다. 그럼에도 불구하고 32세의 이한응은 이를 실행에 옮긴 것이다. 그의 이러한 애국충심에서 이루어진 자결의 소식은 널리 세계에 전파되어 각국 외교계에 커다란 충격을 주었으며, 국내에 전하여서는 온 국민의 심금을 감격과 애통으로 가득하게 하였다. 애국의 화신인 이한응의 유해는 고종의 특별지시와 당시 런던주재 한국 총영사 모건의 노력으로 그 해 7월 해로(海路)로 고국에 귀환되어 관리들과 국민들의 애도 속에 고향인 용인군 이동면 덕성리 금현(金峴)에 모셔졌다. 그의 고결한 인품, 숭고한 행동, 그리고 애국애족의 정신은 길이길이 이 겨레에 전해질 것이다. 이한응의 순국은 을사늑약(1905. 11. 17.)이 체결되기 반년 전이었으며, 조약 후 자결한 민영환·조병세·홍만식·송병선 보다 7-8개월 앞섰고, 해외에서 순사(殉死: 근자에 병사로 확인됨)한 이준 보다는 2년 전의 일이다. 구한말 순국열사 중 최초였다는 점에서 그의 순국은 한층 더 높이 평가된다.

당시 조정에서도 이한응의 절의와 순국을 가상히 여겨 종2품 가선대부(嘉善大夫), 내부협판(內部協辦)에 추증하고 관원을 특파하여 치제(致

祭)하였으며, 장충단(奬忠壇)에 배향(配享)하였다. 1962년 정부에서 순국열사 이한응에게 건국훈장 독립장을 추서하였으며, 1964년 장충단 공원에 그의 순국기념비가 세워져 있다.

이한응은 딸만 하나 있어, 그의 유언대로 사후(死後) 생가의 동생 한승(漢昇)의 둘째아들 상룡(相龍)을 양자로 삼았다.

3 외교활동과 그 의의 _____

(1) 주영 외교관 시기의 한반도를 둘러싼 국제 정세

20세기 초기의 한반도를 둘러싼 국제 정세는 제국주의 시대가 그 절정에 달했던 시기이다. 이 시기에 일본은 서구의 충격을 넘어 서구식 제국주의의 길로 접어듦에 따라 그 발판을 마련하기 위해 한반도에 욕심을 내던 때였다. 이때 우리나라는 19세기 후반 영국과 러시아, 프랑스 등 서구 열강과 정식 수교를 맺으며 정치적인 독립을 대외적으로 알리고자 하였다. 국가안보에 있어서는 외세의 침략에 대해 다른 서구열강을 끌어들여 막으려는 전통적인 이이제이의 외교 정책을 유지하였다. 이러한 조선의 대외 정책으로 인하여 국가 도덕성에 치명타를 입게 되고, 결국 영국·프랑스 등 서구 열강들의 조선에 대한 이해관계가 줄어들자 이들 나라들에게 조선의 독립을 지지하는 입장에서 돌아서게 되는 빌미를 제공하게 된다.

구체적으로 이 시기에 일본은 한국을 침략하여 자기들의 보호국 내지는 식민지로 만들려는 목적을 숨기지 않았다. 이를 위해 1894년 청일전쟁을 일으켜 청군을 조선에서 몰아내게 된다. 그러나 당시의 급변하는 국제 정세가 일본이 순순히 조선을 점령하도록 내버려 두지는 않았다. 북쪽에서 시베리아를 차지하고 연해주를 거쳐 남하하는 제정 러시아 세력이 만주까지 점령하면서 한반도로 그 세력을 급속히 확장해 나가고 있었기 때문이었다. 또 국내적으로는 조선 국민의 반일 감정이 팽배하여 결과적으로 일본의 조선 침략 작업은 일단락되기에 이르렀다.

그 뒤 10년 동안 일본은 제국주의적 야망을 포기하지 않았다. 그래서 국내적으로는 침략전쟁을 수행하기 위한 군국주의 체제로의 전환에 총력을 기울여 나가고, 국외적으로는 제1차 영·일 동맹을 맺는 등 안팎으로 조선을 침략하기 위한 작업을 차근차근 진행해 나갔다. 제1차 영·일 동맹은 이한응이 런던에서 외교관으로 있던 시기인 1902년 일본과 영국 사이에 맺어진 협약으로, 일본이 다른 나라에 앞서 조선에 대한 정치·경제·군사적 간섭권을 가진다는 것을 영국이 보장한다는 내용을 주요 골자로 한 것이다. 이러한 협약을 통하여 일본은 조선에 대한 우선적인 권리를 보장받게 되고, 영국 역시 당시 강대국의 한 축이었던 러시아의 영토 확장에 대한 견제를 꾀할 수 있었던 것이다.

1904년 2월 일본은 러·일 전쟁을 도발하게 된다. 여순항과 봉천 등지에서 러시아군에 기습적인 승리를 거둔 일본군은 대한해협에서 막강한 러시아의 발틱함대마저 물리침으로써 조선 점령의 가장 큰 걸림돌을 제거하는데 성공한다. 러·일 전쟁에서의 승리로 국제적 위상을 높인 일본은, 이듬해 5월에 미국과 가쓰라-테프트 밀약을 맺어 미국의 필리핀 지배를 인정하는 대신 미국으로부터 일본의 조선 지배를 인정받게 된다. 같은 해에 영국과 일본은 제2차 영·일 동맹을 다시 체결하게 된다. 이것은 문자 그대로 영국이 일본의 조선에 있어서의 정치적·군사적 감독권을 인정하여 사실상의 조선의 속국화를 인정하는 것이었다. 이에 따라 일본은 조선을 식민지화 하기위한 모든 작업을 끝마치게 된다.

러·일 전쟁이 발발하기 직전인 1904년 1월 조선정부는 국외중립(局外中立)을 선언하여 어느 나라의 편의도 봐주지 않을 것을 국제적으로 천명하나 각국의 이해관계가 첨예하게 대립되던 한반도에서 이 중립화 방안은 어느 나라에게도 인정받지 못한다.

(2) 영국에서의 외교활동

1901년 3월 조선정부는 유럽국가 중에는 최초로 영국에 공사 민영돈과 참서관 이한응을 파견한다. 그러나 민영돈은 국제적인 외교활동보다는 국내정치에 더 관심을 가지고 있었기 때문에 1904년 2월 본국으로 먼저 귀국하게 된다. 그 후임으로 박영하가 지명되었으나 실제로 영국에는 부임하지 않고 있다가 1905년 9월 외무대신 서리로 임명된다. 그러므로 이한응은 1904년 5월부터 1905년 5월까지 거의 유일하게 유럽에 상주하던 조선의 외교관이며, 조선 정부의 유일한 공식 외교 통로였던 것이다.

이 기간 동안 그는 당시 국제 외교의 중심무대였던 런던에서 신문·잡지 등 가능한 모든 채널을 통하여 한반도 정세에 대한 정보를 수집하여 공사관일지에 기록하게 된다.

공사관 일지에 기록된 주요 사항들을 살펴보면 다음과 같다.

"1904년 1월 21일 목요일
한성(漢城) 발에 의하면 한국(韓國: 대한제국의 약칭임)은 황제가 조칙을 반포하여 정부를 다시 조직하고 한산(閑散)한 아문(衙門)들을 혁파했다고 한다.
한성 발에 의하면 한국 조정은 러시아 조회에 대해 러시아가 한국 군인들이 한국의 변계(邊界)에서 난류(亂流)한 일 등에 대해 간섭할 권리가 없다고 했다 한다."

이 글에서는 마치 조선(혼동의 우려가 있어 한국이라 하지 않고 조선으로 칭한다) 정부가 러시아에 대해서만 간섭권을 제한한 것처럼 보여진다.

그러나 이 날은 조선 정부가 국외중립(局外中立)을 선언한 날이다. 이한응이 이에 대한 본국의 사전 연락을 받았는지 언급하고 있지 않지만, 당시에 통상적으로 전보가 2-3일 걸렸던 점을 감안한다면, 시간적 여유가 충분히 있었음에도 직접적인 의사소통은 없었던 것으로 보인다. 외신 보도만을 인용한 이 글을 통해 보면 그가 이 문제에 대해 본국으로부터 어떠한 사전지식도 직접 전달받지 못했던 것으로 생각된다. 유럽 내의 거의 유일한 공사관에서 홀로 대유럽외교를 책임지다시피 했던 이한응조차 각종 기사를 통하여 간접적으로 조선의 외교정책을 접하는 상황이었다. 그런 바 조선정부의 뜻을 제대로 유럽에 전달할 수 있는 체계적인 외교정책과 통신망이 아직까지 만들어지지 않고 있었다고 가정하여 보기는 어렵지 않을 것이다.

그에 비해 일본은 조선의 국외중립선언에 대해 발 빠른 조치를 취했던 것으로 보인다.

"1904년 1월 23일 토요일
영국 신문에 의하면 일본 정부는 영국·미국·독일 3국의 정부에 서신을 보내, 일본과 러시아의 담판에 관한 일에 대해 일본이 앞으로 다른 나라들의 간여를 불허할 것임을 밝혔다고 한다."

그러나 이한응은 공사관 일지에서 이러한 외신보도에 대해 거의 논평을 가하지 않고 있어 해당 자료만으로는 그의 외교관(外交觀)을 알기 어려운 점이 있다. 영국 공문서보관소에서 이한응과 면담한 영국 외무성 관리들의 기록과 이한응의 메모, 공문 등이 발견되어 단국대학교 동양학연구소에서 2001-2002년 해당 자료를 입수(현재 마이크로필름 보관 중)하

였다. 이한응과 관련된 국내의 기록이 거의 남아있지 않은 상황에서 짐작
컨대, 그가 조선 정부와 긴밀한 협조 하에서 외교활동을 하지는 않았던
것으로 보인다. 그러나 이한응이 조선인으로서는 최초로 외국(영국)에서
4년여 간 거주하며 격동기의 조선을 외부에서 객관적인 시각으로 바라본
점과, 당시의 국제정세 속에서 조선이 가야할 방향을 모색했던 점 등은
주목할 필요가 있다.

(3) 외교활동의 의의

당시의 조선 정부가 영국에 공사 및 참서관을 파견한 것은 '조선의 주
권 독립을 세계에 알리고 승인' 받기 위한 노력의 일환으로 보여진다. 궁
극적으로는 외교적인 수단을 통하여 열강들에 의한 한반도 중립화(국외
중립)를 목표로 한 것이었다.

이한응의 외교활동 역시 이러한 맥락에서 이뤄졌던 것으로 파악된다.
러·일 전쟁이 발발하기 전에 한반도를 기준으로 영국과 일본을 한 축으
로 삼고, 러시아-프랑스를 다른 축으로 삼아 조선의 중립화를 달성하고자
하였던 것이다. 결국 한반도 중립화 방안을 통하여 조선의 주권과 독립,
현상 유지를 위해 영국 정부가 노력해 줄 수 있는지 영국 외무성에 꾸준
히 질의서를 보내며 노력을 하였다.

"영국과 프랑스는 러시아와 일본의 갈등을 해소시키고, 만주와 조선에
서의 그들의 상호 이익을 보장하는 심판관의 역할을 수행해야 한다.
외교적으로 4국 조약(영국, 프랑스, 러시아, 일본)을 맺어서, 한반도에
서 일본이나 러시아로 힘이 쏠릴 경우에 영국과 프랑스는 균형을 다시

복원하는 균형추의 역할을 수행해야만 한다. 그게 동아시아의 평화, 나아가서는 세계평화를 유지하는 길이다."

(이한응이 영국 외무성에 보낸 메모 中)

이한응은 조선의 평화가 유럽의 세력균형과 연관된 문제이기에, 조선의 독립은 극동의 평화만이 아니라 세계의 평화와도 직결된다는 논리를 내세워서 외무성 관리들을 설득시키려고 하였다. 또한 그는 세계의 세력균형이라는 점에서 극동지역에서의 적대적 관계를 설명하였다.

이에 대해 영국 정부는 한반도의 상황이 어떻게 전개될지 모르는 상황에서 조선의 독립을 지지해 달라는 이한응의 요구에 대해 난색을 표명하게 된다. 적대적인 상황 속에서 조선의 독립을 유지하는 것이 어렵고, 주한 영국공사 조던의 정세판단으로는 어느 나라이던 간에 조선의 수도를 먼저 점령하는 국가가 조선의 미래를 좌우할 것이라는 이유에서이다. 즉, 영국은 조선의 주권과 독립을 지지하기는 하지만, 실제적으로는 그런 상태를 고착시키기 위해서 어떠한 물리적인 대응도 어렵다는 것이었다.

실제로 1905년 2월에 일본은 해외에 나가있는 조선의 외교관을 소환하라는 압박을 조선 황제에게 가하게 된다. 이와 같은 제국주의적 흐름을 그 본거지인 영국의 수도 런던에서 뼈저리게 보고 느끼던 이한응은 일개 외교관의 힘으로는 어찌할 수 없음을 깨닫고는 끝내 자결의 길을 택하게 된다.

"오호라 나라의 주권이 없어지고, 사람의 평등을 잃으니 모든 교섭에 치욕이 망극할 따름이다. 진실로 피를 가진 사람이라면 어찌 참고 견디리오. 나라가 장차 무너지고, 온 민족이 남의 노예가 되리라. 구차스럽게 산다는 것은 욕됨만 더할 따름이다. 이 어찌 죽는 것보다 낫겠는가? 죽을 뜻을 매듭지으니 다시 할 말이 없노라."

(이한응의 유서 中)

영국 공사 서리 이한응의 죽음은 1905년 후반 이후의 대외관계에 큰 영향을 미치게 된다. 이한응의 자결 소식을 들은 고종 황제는 일단 파리 주재 공사관 직원 중 한 명을 우선 런던으로 파견하기로 결정한다. 그러나 재외 한국공사관을 폐쇄하려는 일본의 압력에 굴복하여 공사 임명을 포기하게 되고 은밀히 파리주재 공사관 직원 1명을 런던으로 보내지만, 본국으로부터의 임명절차가 없는 것을 이유로 영국 정부로부터 공사 업무를 인계받지 못한다. 결국 같은 해 7월에 런던 뿐만이 아니라 파리·베를린·워싱턴에 있던 공사관마저 폐쇄하고 그 곳에 근무하던 외국인 고문들도 해임되기에 이른다. 이로부터 한 달 후 조선의 독립조항이 삭제된 제 2차 영·일 동맹이 성립되어 영국은 조선에 있어서의 일본의 우월적 지위를 인정하게 된다.

수만리 떨어진 이역 땅에서 민영돈 공사를 보좌해 가면서 외교 업무를 집행하는 청년 외교관 이한응은 항상 불안한 환경에 처하여 있는 조국의 미래를 근심하는 한편 변화무쌍한 국제정세를 통찰하였다. 그러면서도 그는 자기수양에도 끊임없는 노력을 기울였는데, 이는 조국에 이바지하는 길은 먼저 자기 개인의 인격완성이 있고서야만 개척할 수 있다는 믿음을 가지고 있었기 때문이었던 것이다.

따라서 이한응의 런던 주재 4년여 간의 근면하고 충실한 생활 자세와 태도는 영국의 외교계와 일반사회는 물론 외국의 주영 외교관들에게도 많은 존경과 추앙을 받았던 바, 을사년 5월에 선생의 순절을 본국 정부에 통지한 영국의 런던주재 한국총영사 모건의 아래와 같은 보고문 중의 일

부분만으로도 가히 알 수가 있다.

"5월 12일 런던 주재 한국 공사 서리 이한응이 자결했습니다. 그 분은 지난 몇 달 동안 극동전쟁(러일전쟁)에 대한 일로 상심을 많이 했고, 한국의 이익 관계로 더욱 노심초사 했습니다. 본국으로부터 반갑지 않은 소식을 들을 때마다 비분강개 했습니다. 이 선생은 조선에서 가장 공정정대한 분으로서 학문에 부지런한 품성을 발휘했고, 근면했던 모범적인 분이었습니다. 그러므로 영국에 주재해 있는 동안 여러 가지 불리한 환경에 처해 있으면서도 그 국제적 지위를 잘 보존하였습니다. 따라서 영국의 외무부나 일반사회에서는 다른 열국의 외교 대표인들과 조금도 차이 없이 선생을 우대하여 왔습니다."

이한응의 죽음은 한국과 일본 간에 보호조약이 체결되기 이전에 이루어짐으로 인해서 순국 제1호로 받아들여지게 된다. 이는 1905년 11월에 체결된 보호조약에 울분을 참지 못하고 자결한 민영환 등 수명의 지사들보다 더욱 빠른 것이었다. 이한응은 머나먼 이국에서 조국의 밝지 못한 미래, 망국의 조짐을 예견하고 자결이라는 최후의 수단으로 항거한 최초의 한국인이었던 것이다.

또한 이한응은 한국인으로서는 최초로 서양에서 4년여 동안 장기 체류한 인물이다. 그를 통하여 한국의 대 서양인식을 규명하는 열쇠를 제공하여 줄 수도 있을 것이다. 뿐만 아니라 영국 외무성을 상대로 독자적인 외교활동을 벌이는 가운데 조선이 열강의 틈바구니에서 살아남을 수 있는 길은 한반도 중립화안 임을 간파하고 이를 제안했을 뿐만 아니라, 그 방안이 탁월했다는 점에서 높이 평가된다.

4 맺음말 ──────────────────

필자의 과문인지는 몰라도 지금까지 순국열사 이한응에 관한 본격적인 연구는 거의 전무한 상태인 듯하다.

이한응은 외교관으로서 최초로 순국한 열사일 뿐만 아니라, 한반도 중립화 방안의 설계자로 높이 평가할 만하다. 유길준 등을 비롯한 극소수의 인물들이 한반도 중립화 방안을 언급한 적이 있지만, 이한응의 한반도 중립화 방안은 이들보다 구체적일 뿐만 아니라 상당한 설득력을 지니고 있다는 점에서 주목할 필요가 있다. 그러므로 영국 외무성에서는 영일동맹이 체결되었음에도 불구하고, 이한응의 한반도 중립화 방안을 한동안 면밀하게 검토한 적이 있었다. 이로써 보건데 그의 한반도 중립화 방안은 설득력과 함께 의의가 있는바 높이 평가된다. 뿐만 아니라 오늘날의 상황과 연관 지어 볼 때 이한응의 한반도 중립화 방안은 21C 통일지향의 밑거름이 될 수 있을 것이다. 또한 그는 한국인 최초로 서양에 장기 체류한 인물로서 한국의 대 서양인식을 규명하는데 열쇠 역할을 한다고 본다. 그리고 외교관으로서 국제정치에 대한 탁월한 식견은 국제화·세계화 시대를 지향하는 오늘날과 비교할 때 선구적일 뿐만 아니라 본보기로 삼을 만하다.

끝으로 우리에게 남겨진 과제를 언급하는 것으로 이 글을 마무리 하고자 한다.

지금까지는 민씨 척족인 민영환이 순국 제1호로써 우리에게 받아들여지고 있다. 그러나 머나먼 영국에서 우리나라를 둘러싼 구미 열강과 일본의 야욕을 목도하고, 외교관으로서 이를 저지하기위해 최선을 다하다가 자신의 한계를 절감하고 비통한 심정으로 자결한 이한응 열사가 민영환

보다 더 선각자적인 입장에 있음을 인정해야 할 것이다. 이러한 이한응 열사의 객관적인 통찰력과 외교적인 노력은 그가 국제화 시대에 앞선 인물이라는 것을 보여준다는 점과, 자결로 시대적 흐름에 항거하고자 한 최초의 인물이라는 점 등에서, 역사적 중요성과 함께 오늘날의 젊은이들에게 본받을 점과 많은 시사점을 제시해 준다고 하겠다. 따라서 순국열사 이한응을 교과서에 게재하여 널리 알리는 것이 급선무라고 생각된다. 그리고 이한응 열사는 용인시, 더 나아가서는 우리나라의 자랑스러운 인물임으로 그를 널리 알리고 추모하기 위해 공원조성 등 기념사업이 필요하다고 본다. 뿐만 아니라 방송·신문 등 매스컴을 통해 그를 제대로 조명 평가할 필요가 있다.

이역만리 영국 땅에서 망해가는 나라를 살리기 위해 홀로 열과 성을 다해 노력하다 순국한 이한응 선생을 생각하면 말로 표현할 수 없는 존경과 함께 가슴 저미는 아픔을 느낀다.

자 료

영국 공문서 보관소(PRO) 관련 자료
순국열사이한응선생추모회 편, 『殉國烈士李漢應先生遺史』, 문예홍보사, 1957.
이민섭 정리, 「순국 열사 이한응 선생의 생애와 사상」, 1995.
『全義李氏族譜』

논 저

Ku Dae Yeol, *A KOREAN DIPLOMAT IN LONDON: YI HANEUNG AND ANGLO-KOREAN RELATIONS.*
구대열, 「이한응과 한-영 관계」, 『성곡논총』 16, 1985.
송재용, 「구한말 최초의 순국열사 이한응」, 『용인향토문화연구』 제6집, 용인향토문화연구회, 2005.

※

이한응의 당질인 이상준(이한응의 큰아버지인 이만호의 손자)에 의하면, 이한응은 15세 이전까지 큰아버지인 이만호에게 한학을 배웠다고 한다. 그리고 이한응은 한때 수원에서 살았던 적도 있으며, 충북 음성에 있는 처가에서도 잠시 살았다고 하는데 자세히 알 수는 없다고 한다.

한편, 이한응의 딸은 5~6세 때 죽었다고 한다. 이한응의 묘는 고종의 명으로 국가와 일가친척들이 돈을 모아 지금의 묘지(덕성리)을 샀다고 한다. 원래 전의 이씨의 선산은 남사면 완장리에 있어 선대 묘가 대부분 이곳에 있는데, 이한응의 묘만 덕성리에 있다고 한다. 그리고 전의 이씨는 화산리에 집성촌을 이루고 살았는데, 묘지 관리 관계로 이상준의 가족만 덕성리에서 거주하고 있으며, 이한응이 자결한 뒤 보내온 돈으로 현재 산업도로가 나 있는 곳에 땅을 사두었는데, 이상준이 그 땅에서 나오는 돈으로 묘지를 관리했었다고 한다.

자료편

자료편 서문

이한응 관련 자료는 ① 순국열사이한응선생 추모회에서 1957년에 출
간한 『순국열사이한응선생유사』, ②손자인 이민섭 동국대 명예교수가
1995년에 정리한 「순국열사 이한응 선생의 생애와 사상」, ③이한응이 작
성한 「공사관일지」(영국신문에 실린 각국과 극동에 관한 정보를 단순히
취합하여 공식적으로 작성한 것이 대부분임), ④이한응 관련 영국 외무성
자료(이한응이 작성한 청원서 및 이한응에 대한 영국인이 남긴 평가 등이
수록) 등이 있다. 이 밖에 靑柳南冥의 『이조5백년사』, 김영하의 『국사연
구』, 서울대 국사연구실의 『국사개설』 등 극히 일부의 국사개설서 및 국
사사전 등에 간단하게 소개되어 있는 정도이다.

여기서는 2001, 2002, 2005년 세 차례에 걸쳐 자료조사를 했던 영국 공
문서보관소 자료를 중심으로 엮었다.

친필유서

영국공문서보관소 소장
이한응 관련 자료

4, Trebovir Road,
Earls Court,
London, s.w. January 15 1904.

Sir,

I have the honour to inform you that I am authorized by my Government to bring to the notice of the British Foreign Office of the circumstances now existing in Corea, and I hope to convey this matter in an interview to be favoured at your early convenience.

I have the honour to be,
Sir,
your obedient,
humble servant,
Yi Han Eung.

F. A. Campbell Esquire
&c.   &c.   &c.

4. Trebovir Road,
Earls Court,
London, s.w. January 20 1904.

His Lordship,
　The Most Hon. the Marquees of Lansdowne K.G.
the Principal Secretary of State for Foreign Affairs.

My Lord,
　　I have the honour to inform your lordship that I have received a telegraphic instruction from His Majesty, the Emperor of Corea, my Sovereign to ask the favour of His Britannic Majesty's Government to give a fresh guarantee for the Corean affairs concerning the present crisis in the Far East as well as for the possible outbreak of the Russo-Japanese War in the near future, as in the following Memorandum.
　　I have further the honour to assure your Lordship that such a benevolent action of the British Government will produce a best means of securing the political position of the Corean Government and of promoting the cordial friendship of our two countries to an advanced stage. I avail myself of this opportunity to renew to your Lordship the assurance of my highest consideration.
　　I have the honour to be, Sir,
　　　your Lordship's Most humble, obedient
　　　　servant. Yi Han Eung.

Memorandum

(1) To protect the independence, sovereignty, integrity and privileges of Corea according to the feature of Anglo-Japanese Treaty.

(2) To prevent any aggressive power from taking the control of the Corean Government in any respects at the present moment as well as in the future.

(3) To prevent any aggressive power from bringing troops into the Corean interior, either in open manner or otherwise, without any serious disturbance or riot which threatens the lives and properties of foreigners therein.

(4) If there be any disturbance in any part of Corea, the Corean Government must have first and full duty to restore order in consequence of its sovereignty.

(5) In case of Russo-Japanese war taking place, the British Government will come to understanding with different powers before or on the outbreak of the said war, and try its utmost to preserve the independence, sovereignty, integrity and privileges of Corea as they are now, on whichever side the victory may be decided.

4, Trebovir Road,
Earls Court,
London, S.W. January 2 2, 1904.

His Lordship,
The Most Hon. the Marquees of Lansdowne, K.G.
The Principal Secretary of State for Freign Affairs.

My Lord,
I have the honour to inform your lordship that I have just received a telegraphic instruction from my Government to communicate with His Britannic Majesty's Government the following declaration:

"Vu les complications que ont surgés entre la Russie et le Japone et au les difficultés que semblent rencontrer les negotiateurs a amener une solution pacifique le gouvernement Coréen par ordre de Sa Majesté l'empereur declare qu'il a pris la ferme resolution d'observer la plus stricte neutralité quel que soit le resultat les pourparler actuellement engages entre les dites puissances, et Sa Majesté l'empereur compte en cette occasion sur le concourse amical de toutes les puissances."

I have the honour to be,
with highest consideration,
sir,
your Lordship's obedient,
humble servant.
Yi Han eung.

Jan: 27: 1904

Sir,

Draft
Yi Han Eung.

I have the honour
to acknowledge with
thanks the receipt
of your note
of the 22nd instant
in which, ~~by direction~~
~~of your Gov't.,~~ you,
state, under instructions,
~~Communicate to me~~
a ~~declaration of~~
the Corean Gov't
that ~~attitude~~ ~~which~~
they have resolved
upon the strictest neutrality
to ~~adopt with~~

F.O.　21

Jan: 27: 1904.

Draft
Yi Han Eung

Sir,

I have the honour
~~to~~ acknowledge with
thanks the receipt
of your note
of the 22nd instant
in which, ~~by direction~~
~~of your Gov't~~., you
State, under instructions,
~~Communicate to me~~
~~a declaration of~~
the Corean Gov't
~~that~~ ~~attitude~~ which
they have resolved
observe the strictest neutrality
to ~~adopt~~ ~~with~~
whatever may be the result of the
~~regard to the difficulties~~
negotiations between Japan and Russia
~~now existing~~ ~~between F.M.~~

F. O.

Jan. 28 · 1904

Draft
Yi Han Eung.

Sir,

I have the honour
to acknowledge the
receipt of your note
of the 20th instant,
~~enclosing~~ ,, 83
a ~~memo~~ ~~setting~~
relative to the
~~forth the terms of a guarantee~~
it is suggested by
which ~~your~~ the Corea Govt.
~~Have a guarantee~~ ~~should be given by~~
~~request~~ ~~that~~ H. M. Govt.
~~will~~ give with regard
to Corea —
The holicy

Draft

Yi Han Eung

70   27 January 1904

(Ref his 22 Jan/04)

Corean Neutrality in event
of war between Japan & Russia

Thanks for his note of 22 Jan/04

of H. M. Gov't in
respect of Corea
may be sufficiently
gathered from the
Anglo-Japanese Agreement
and they ~~cannot~~ are not prepared //
~~attempt at a~~
~~moment like the~~
~~present~~ to supplement
that Agreement by
a further ~~understanding~~ engagement /
such as the Corean Gov't
apparently

apparmtly desire.

4, Trebovir Road,
Earls Court,
London, S.W. February 4. 1904.

Sir,

I have the honour to inform you that I have received a message from my government to communicate to the British Foreign Office, and I hope to convey this matter in an interview to be favoured at your early convenience.

I have the honour to be,
Sir,
your most obedient,
humble servant.
Yi Han Eung.

F. A. Campbell Esq.
&c.   &c.   &c.

Yi Han Eung.

7.0   9 February 19.04

Ref his 4 Feb/04

Comm~ from Corean Govt.

Prefers receipt in writing.
interview could be arranged later
for explanation of necessary.

Earls Court,
London, S.W. February 13, 1904.

Sir,

I have the honour to acknowledge the receipt of your answer of the 9th inst. to my note of the 4th in which I asking you for an interview to communicate to the British Foreign Office the message I received from my Government, and I beg to state that it requires further instructions to bring this matter to your notice.

I have the honour to be,
Sir,
your most obedient,
humble servant.

Yi Han Eung.

F. A. Campbell Esq.
&c.   &c.   &c.

Yi Han. Eung

7.0   9 February 1904.

Ref his 14 Feb/04

Comm from Corean Govt.

Prefers receipt in writing,
interview could be arranged later
for explanation if necessary

4. Trebovir Road,
Earls Court,
London, February 13, 1904.
S.W.

Sir,

I have the honour to acknowledge the receipt of your answer of the 9th inst. to my note of the 4th in which I asking you for an interview to communicate to the British Foreign Office the message I received from my Government, and I beg to state that it requires further instructions to bring this matter to your notice.

I have the honour to be,
sir,
your most obedient,
humble servant.

Yi Han Eung.

F. A. Campbell Esq.
 do.   do.   do.

R 15/16 } February 1904
(Ref FO. Feb—4)

Message from Corean Govt
Further instrns required reifg
commn to H.M.Govt

It is rather
doubtful what this
note means; but
it does not appear
to require an answer
in.
I suppose he means
he needs further instructions
before he can make
his communication
JAC

4, Trebovir Road,
Earls Court,
London, February 25, 1904.
S.W.

Sir,

I have the honour to inform you that I have an opinion to express to you in connexion with the Corean neutrality being the subject of the Russian note to the powers, and of the reported Japanese treaty with Corea concerning Japan's military operations, and of which I hope to convey to you in an earliest moment.

If you would be so good as to grant me an interview at your earliest convenient hour, I shall be very pleased to call upon you at the Foreign Office.

I have the honour to be,
Sir,
your obedient,
humble servant,
Yi Han Eung.

F. A. Campbell Esq.
&c.   &c.   &c.

<u>The Russian Note to the
Powers. Corean neutrality.
Coreo- Japanese Agreement</u>.
Has an opinion to express
resp + requests interview.

Q^d ack y^r receipt
and request him to
make the communication
in writing in the first
instance in order that
it may receive due
consideration.   H.

(For Mr Campbell's signature)
134 Corea Feb. 29 /04

4. Trebovir Road.
Earls Court.
London, February 29. 1904.
S.W.

Sir,

I have the honour to inform you that I addressed a note to you on the 25th instant asking you to favour me an interview in order to express my opinion on the Corean neutrality being the subject of the Russian note to the powers, and the reported Japanese treaty with Corea, and herewith I beg to say that I was informed that the said treaty was negotiating between Japan and Corea, and, I think now it is too late to express my opinion on that subject.

My opinion was to get a guarantee both from Russia and Japan and to preserve our independence and foreign interests (includes Japanese) in Corea whatever may be the result of the Russo-Japanese war, and if we were in the position to take such a step we should have come to understanding with the British Government.

I have further the honour to express my satisfaction that the conclusion of the Corean-Japanese treaty will, no doubt, furnish a

a

fresh guarantee for the permanent
peace in the Far East and the thorough
understanding between Japan and
Corea,

    I have the honour to be,
   With high consideration,
      sir,
   your most obedient,
     humble servant,
      Yi Han Eung.

F. A. Campbell Esq.
   etc.   etc. etc.

osbooket

F.0. 31

March 3 1904.

Oft.
Hon Euoy,
Treborir Road,
Earls Court.
S. W.

Sir,
I have the
honour to ack. the
receipt of your Note
of the 29th ultimo,
in which you state
that you now
consider it too late
to give an opinion
relative to the Note addressed
by the Russian Gout
to

to the Powers resp.

the neutrality of

Corea; ~~& express'~~

~~your satisfaction~~

and ~~that~~ the conclusion

of the treaty between

Corea & Japan. will

no doubt furnish a

fresh guarantee for

permanent peace in

the Far East.

JdB

I much regret
your previous Note
the 25th was not
answered earlier, but
the reply was on th
point of being desp
when your Note of
29th was received.

4, Trebovir Road,
Earls Court,
London, April 19.   1904.
S.W.

His Lordship,
The Most Hon. the Marquess of Lansdowne, K.G.
The Principal Secretary of State for Foreign Affairs.

My Lord,

I have the honour to inform your lordship that I having received a telegram from my Government in which instructing me to convey to your Lordship the sincere thanks of His Majesty the Emperor of Corea, my Sovereign, for the loyal service rendered by the English Marines in extinguishing the fire at the Imperial Palace at Seoul on the 14th instant.

I avail myself of this opportunity to renew to your lordship the assurance of my highest consideration.

I have the honour to be,

Sir,
your Lordship's most humble,
obedient servant,

Yi Han Eung.

F. O.

April. 23. 1904.

Draft.

Yi Han Eung.

Copy to Admlty
with Yi Han Eung.
April: 19.

Sir,

I have the honour to acknowledge the receipt of your note of the 19th instant in which you convey the thanks of H.M. the Emperor of Corea for the services rendered by British marines in extinguishing the recent fire at the Imperial Palace at Seoul.

I have the honour

to express the

Satisfaction of H. M.

Gov.t *at learning* that the

Marines were able

t h of assistance

on that occasion

Hb

F.O. April. 23, 1904

(his of apr 19)

Assistance rendered by
British marines in
extinguishing fire at the
Imperial Palace at Seoul

satisfaction that they
were able to help.

✓ P.L. Apr. 25/04.
Copy to Admiralty with
Yi Han Eung's letter of
April 19.

12.2. Corea

4, Trebovir Road,
Earls Court,
London, October 7.   1904.
S.W.

Sir,

With reference to my request to the Foreign Office on the 21st of September I most earnestly beg you to be so good enough as to suggest His Lordship, the Most Hon. the Marquess of Lansdowne, K.G. to despatch a telegraphic message, if the inquiries were made otherwise, to His Britannic Majesty's Minister at Seoul in his convenience and instruct His Excellency to strongly urge the Corean Government to send a Minister to London as soon as possible.

Herewith I trouble you again with this request in view of the urgent necessity of a Minister in London, and of the possible unfavourable weather for the voyage in the approaching winter-season.

I have the honour to be,
With highest consideration,
Sir,
your most obedient,
humble servant,
Yi Han Eung.

C. H. Montgomery Esq.
&c. &c. &c.

R 7 Oct 1904

(Ref his 21 Sept.)

Appt of Corean 'Minister in London

asks FO. to make representations to Corean Govt

Sir J. Jordan has been written to privately to ask whether he can make inquiries as to the intentions of the Corean Govt in regard to the appt of a Corean Minister

443 Corea.

he is aware we have ~~not~~ in communication with H.M. Minister at Seoul on the subject and must await his answer.

FB

K2.

Aftt. Yi Han Eung Oct. 12 1904

Draft
to Han Eung

F.O

Oct: 12 1904

Sir,

I have the honour
to ack. the receipt
of your ~~letter~~ note of the
7th instant, suggesting
that telegraphic instructions
should be sent to HM's
Minister at Seoul to
urge the Corean Gov't
to appoint a Minister
at this Court without
delay.

As you are aware

M. L

I laid before the
~~express~~ of Lansdowne the
IS. addressed by you
Mr. Montgomery on the

I. Sun

I ~~have~~ communicated
some time ago
with Sir J. Jordan on

it
the subject and ~~his~~
would therefore be advisable to
~~reply~~ ~~must be~~ awaited
his answer
before any further

Steps ~~can be taken by~~
are taken
~~H Go~~ in the matter.

FHL

F.O.

Jan: 9 1904

Draft.

Ye Han Eung

Sir,

I laid before The King
my Sovereign, your note of
the 4th inst. conveying to
he the intelligence of
the death of Her Majesty
the Dowager Empress of
Corea Meung Hiun,
which took place at
Seoul on the 2nd inst.,

The

The King commands
me to request you to be
as good as to convey to
H. M. the Emperor of Corea
His sincere condolences on
the bereavement which
His Imperial Majesty and
His Family have sustained
on this mournful occasion.

Fab

Yi Han Using

F.O. January 9 1904

(Aus: 4ᵏ Last)

Death of Dowager Empress
of Korea.

The King desires his
sincere condolences
conveyed to Emperor.

4, Trebovir Road,
Earls Court,
London, S.W. January 20 1904.

His Lordship,
    The Most Hon, the Marquees of Lansdowne K.G.
The Principal Secretary of State for Foreign Affairs.

My Lord,
        I had conveyed to His Majesty, The
Emperor of Corea, my sovereign the sincere condolences of His Majesty, The King of Great
Britain and Ireland and Emperor of India
for the death of Her Late Majesty, The Dowager
Empress of Corea, Miung Hiun; and I am authorized by His Majesty, The Emperor of Corea,
my sovereign to request your Lordship to
be so good as to convey His sincere thanks
to His Majesty, The King-Emperor for His
kind sympathy displayed on that mournful
occasion.
                I have the honour to be,
        With high Consideration
                    Sir,
            your Lordship's most obedient,
                    humble servant,
                        Yi Han Eung.

20 January 1904
22
(Anc. 9.)

Death of the Dowager-Empress
of Corea

The Emperor's thanks for
His Majesty's condolences

The King ✓

CH.

Corea

4. Trebovir Road,
Earls Court,
London, S.W. May 25. 1904.

His Lordship.
The Most Hon. the Marquess of Lansdowne, K.G.
The Principal Secretary of State for Foreign affairs.

My Lord,
I have the honour to inform your Lordship
that I having received an autograph letter from
His Majesty the Emperor of Corea to His Majesty
the King announcing the death of Her late Majesty
the Dowager Empress Miung-hurn, which took place
at Kiung-woon Palace at Seoul on the 2nd of
January last, and herewith I have the honour
of forwarding the same to your Lordship to be so
good enough as to present it to His Majesty the
King, and thus I shall feel much appreciated.
I avail myself of this opportunity to renew
to your Lordship the assurance of my highest
consideration.

I have the honour to be,
Sir,
your Lordship's most humble,
obedient servant.

Yi Han Eung.

R 25 26 May 1904

Death of the Dowager
Empress of Corea.

Tris. Letter from the
Emperor of Corea to The
King announcing.

The King

Sipur 22.
Prepare suitable.
Reply to The Emperor's
Letter.

Acknowledge this note

FWb

May. 26

Corea.

Draft.

Yi Han Eung

F. O.,

May 28 , 1904.

Sir

I have the honour to acknowledge the receipt of *your* Note of the 25th instant , in which you transmit a Letter from H.M. the Emperor of Corea ——————

to the King notifying the death of Her Majesty the Dowager Empress of Corea

and I beg leave to acquaint *you* in reply, that I have not failed to lay this letter before His Majesty.

I have, &c.

W.m

DRAFT.

Yi Han Eung.

F. O., *May 28* 1904

(Ans. **25**th)

Death of the Dowager Empress of Corea

Acknowledges receipt of Letter from

the Emperor of Corea

notifying

4, Trebovir Road,
E——t-Court,
London, November 7. 1904
S.W.

The Corean Chargé d'affaires presents his
compliments to His Lordship, the Most Hon.
the Marquess of Lansdowne, K.G., and with the
deepest sorrow to acquaint His Lordship that
Her Imperial Highness, the Crown Princess of
Corea died at Seoul at 8 o'clock p.m. on the 5th
instant.

7} Nov 1904

<u>Death of Crown Princess of Corea</u>
Reports.

Nov: 12

Acknowledge
Suitably

(The Kings reports
have been telegraphed)

FB

WM
Nov 9

Corea

Draft

Yi Han Eung.

n Chargé d'Affaires.)

F.O.

November 12 1904.

Sir,

I have the honour to acknowledge the receipt of your Note of the
7th Instant, in which you announce the
death of H.I.H. the Crown Princess of
Corea, which took place at Seoul on the
5th Instant.

The King, my Sovereign, had
already learnt the sad intelligence by
telegraph from H.M.Minister at Seoul,
and H.M. at once despatched a message
of sympathy direct to H.M. the Emperor
of Corea.

I ~~trust that I may be permit~~
present to
~~ted to take~~ the opportunity of expres-

~~Ping~~ the feelings of regret with which

H.M.G. have received the news of H.

I.H.'s death.

4. Trebovir Road,
Earls Court,
London, November 15 1904
S.W.

His Lordship,
The Most Hon. the Marquess of Lansdowne, K.G.
The Principal Secretary of State for Foreign Affairs.

My Lord,
I have the honour to acknowledge the receipt of your Lordship's reply to my note of the 7th instant, and am much impressed to learn that His Majesty the King had been so gracious enough as to despatch a direct message of sympathy to His Majesty the Emperor of Corea on being informed of the death of Her Imperial Highness the Crown Princess of Corea.

I am also much appreciated for the kind sympathy of His Majesty's Government; and I shall lose no time in conveying the same to my Government.

I have the honour to be,
With highest consideration,
Sir,
your Lordship's most obedient,
humble servant,
Yi Han Eung.

D. 15
R 17   Nov. 1904

(Ref his 7th inst)

Death of Crown Princess of

Corea.

appreciation of H.M's sympathy

The King V

4. Trebovir Road,
Earls Court,
London, September 24 1904.
S.W.

Sir,

I have the honour to acknowledge the receipt of your kind letter of yesterdays date and am much glad to be informed that inquiries have been made to His Britannic Majesty's Minister at Seoul to ascertain from the Corean Government what their intentions are with regard to the appointment of a Minister at St. James's Court.

I most earnestly wish that we shall soon have a Minister in London, and thus it will give us the better means of pursuing our diplomatic course and the promotion of our mutual interests.

I beg you to be so good enough as to convey this idea to His Lordship the Most Hon. the Marquess of Lansdowne, K.G., and thus much appreciated.

I have the honour to be,
With highest consideration,
sir,
your most obedient
humble servant,
Yi Han Eung.

C. H. Montgomery Esq.
&c.   &c.   &c.

can make enquiry?

FO 22 Sep/04

Yi Han Eung informed Privately

Sept 23.

4, Trebovir Road,
Earls Court,
London, February 22 1905.
S.W.

Dear sir,

~ Would you do me the favour and allow me to send a message, concerning my statement which I made to you on the 8th instant, to the Corean Government through the medium of His Majesty's Consul at Chifu, and on receiving reply through the same medium I should like to submit a memorandum to His Lordship, the Most Hon. the Marquess of Lansdowne, K.G.

If you think it inconvenient for you to allow me to send a message through the medium of His Majesty's Consul, could you tell me the name of an English Gentleman at Chifu to whom I can send a message and cause the same to be sent to the Corean Postmaster-General by post. In this case I want you to send a short message to His Majesty's Consul at Chifu to instruct the same gentleman to send the same message to the Corean Postmaster-General, sent by post.

I should like to send such a message without being known to the public at Seoul and as for the despatch of the same over here should be sent by a private person as well. I await your kind advice.

I am, sir,

yours faithfully

Yi Han Eung.

Walter L. F. G. Langley, C. B.

do. do. do.

Yi Han Eung

22 February 1905

Message to his Gov't.

Wishes to send it through H. M. Consul at Chefoo

Yi Han Eung when he called here on the 8th was chiefly occupied with the probabilities which events might bring to Corea, and he particularly wishes to telegraph his _____ to Corea

... any light ... at Chefoo through whom he could communicate with his Gov't. Please [I W.] express regret that we are unable to assist him in the manner proposed as it w'd be contrary to our practice.

(I have little doubt his object is as you suggest the nestled us before about urging to app' of [Corean] [counsels] who was a little anti-Japanese _____.)

Feb. 22/2

Apr. 23. 05

... views on that subject to his Gov't. His object in telegraphing via H. M. Consul at Chefoo may be to communicate with his Gov't. without his message coming to the knowledge of the Japanese.

I might let him know privately that it would be contrary to our practice to telegraph for him through H. M. Consul and that we are unable to

To:
Mr. Yi Han Eung

Copy:

23 Feb

is desire to communicate
th his gov't through H. B. M.
sul at Chifu or a
stish subject. Regrets
ability to comply.

February 23, 1905.

Dear Mr. Yi Han Eung,

I have submitted

for the consideration of

the Under Secretary of State

the suggestion contained in

letter of yesterday

with the Corean Government — to comply with this

through the medium request With regard to your attention
of His Majesty's Consul at I am afraid that suggestion We could not recommend

China any British subject at

I am to Express China through them a

regret that we are message might be sent,

unable to assist you in and the Foreign Office would

proposed

the manner as it would in any case not be in a

be contrary to our practice position to send instructions

to a private individual even

4. Trebovir Road.
Earls Court.
London, February 24. 1905.

Sir,

I have the honour to inform you that I having to-day despatched a message to the Corean Government concerning my statement which I made to you on the 8th instant for an instruction in order to bring the matter to the notice of the British Government

In view of the alleged Russian Peace Terms, which was chiefly Concerned to the Corean Independence which was guaranteed by the Anglo-Japanese Treaty of 1902, January 30th, was telegraphed by Reuter's correspondent in St. Petersburg and was published in all the London Newspapers on the 22nd instant, I beg to call your attention to take my statement abovementioned as an official step, and as for the Memorandum which I referred to in our interview will be followed as soon as I shall have received instructions from my Government.

I wish you would be so good enough as to lay this before His Lordship, the Most Hon. the Marquess of Lansdowne. K.G., and thus much appreciated.

I wish you further would do me the favour and appoint a date for an interview in the early part

of next week, and thus I can bring this matter
little earlier than on the usual Reception Day.

    I have the honour to be,
   With highest consideration,
      Sir,
     your most obedient,
      humble servant.
        Yi Han Eung.

Walter L. F. G. Langley, C.B.

  do.   do.   do.

4. Trebovir Road,
Earls Court,
London, February 24. 1905.
S.W.

Dear Sir,

I have duly received your answer of yesterday's date to my note of the 22nd of instant and I thoroughly understand that you are not in the position to comply with my request.

I wish you to be so good enough as to convey this to Mr. Campbell, and thus much obliged.

I am, Sir,
Yours faithfully
Yi Han Eung.

Walter L. F. G. Langley, C.B.

Yi Han bung

D 24?
R 25? Feb 1905

(Ref P.O. Feb. 23)

Transmission of message to his Govt
through H.M. Consul at Chefoo.

Understands that his request
cannot be complied with.

4. Trebovir Road,
Earls Court,
London, S.W. March 3, 1905.

His lordship,
The Most Hon. the Marquess of Lansdowne, K.G.
The Principal Secretary of State for Foreign Affairs.

My lord,
I have the honour to inform your lordship that I had took the opportunity of coming round to the Foreign Office on the 8th ultimo and had a conversation with Mr Langley on the subject of preserving the independence and the integrity of the Corean Empire as expressed in the Anglo-Japanese Treaty of 1902, January the 30th, as Japan is so far successful in this present war,

I had intended to present a memorandum to your lordship for the above statement, but before that taken place, there was the rumour of the alleged Russian Peace Terms with Japan which was emanating from St. Petersburg and was published in all the London Newspapers on the 22nd ultimo, which was so seriously concerned to the independence and the integrity of the Corean Empire guaranteed by the Anglo-Japanese Treaty of 1902, January, the 30th, therefore I addressed a note to Mr Langley on the 24th ultimo concerning the said rumour and further request him to take my statement which I made to him on the 8th ultimo as an official step, and then there came another rumour

2-1883. 7-1

from Washington on the 25th ultimo concerning the
alleged Japanese Peace Terms with Russia which
was so seriously concerned to the independence
and the integrity of the Corean Empire as the alleged
Russian Peace Terms.

This being the case, I despatched a message to the
Corean Government on the 24th ultimo concerning
My statement made to Mr Langley on the 8th ultimo
and the alleged Russian Peace Terms with Japan, and,
then another on the 27th ultimo concerning the alleged
Japanese Peace Terms with Russia in the following
sense:- "So far, Japan is successful in this present
war, and I believe that this will be the result at the
end, therefore it would be wise for the Corean Govern
ment to consider the question of preserving the
independence and the integrity of the Corean Empire
by means of anglo Japanese Treaty. This treaty was
concluded between Great Britain and Japan for the
maintenance of the independence and the integrity
of the Chinese and Corean Empires, so I think it is
adviceable for the Corean Government to communicate with the British Government to render its
support and preserve the independence and the
integrity of the Corean Empire according to anglo
Japanese Treaty of 1902 January

event of the Russian success. Great Britain is the only power to give weight in this matter." p.S. "According to the alleged Russian Peace Terms with Japan which was telegraphed from St. Petersburg and was published in all the London newspapers on the 22nd instant, the Article I expressing that "Corea to be placed under Japanese sugerainty." This article is so seriously concerned to the independence and the integrity of the Corean Empire guaranteed by the Anglo-Japanese Treaty of 1902, January, the 30th therefore I am communicating with the British Government concerning the said Russian Peace Terms. Instruct me to communicate further with the British Government."

I despatched another message to the Corean Government on the 27th ultimo concerning the alleged Japanese Peace Terms with Russia, which was emanating from Washington and was also published in the London Evening newspapers on the 26th ultimo in the following sense:- "According to the alleged Japanese Peace Terms with Russia, which was emanating from Washington and was also published in the London Evening Newspapers on the 28th instant, the Article III expressing that "Russia shall recognize Japanese influence as supreme" and such as clause and

Japanese Peace Terms, the matter is very serious for the independence and the integrity of the Corean Empire, please instruct me to communicate with the British Goverment."

On the 28th ultimo I received the following telegram from my Government :- "I approve your view on the situation. As for the attitude of the British Government towards the Corean affairs is most impressive from the beginning, and this is the fortune of the nation. As for the question of preserving the independence and the integrity of the Corean Empire, you come to understanding with the British Government so as to insert in the coming Russo-Japanese Peace Treaty an article duly guaranteeing the independence and the integrity of the Corean Empire." On receiving the above instructions from my Government, herewith I have the honour to present to your lordship the accompanied Memorandum for the consideration of the British Government towards the Corean affairs concerning the present situation.

I have the honour to be,
With highest Consideration,
Sir,
Your lordships obedient
humble servant.

Memorandum.

(1) So far, Japan is successful in this present war, therefore I most earnestly wish that the independence and the integrity of the Corean Empire would be secured and maintained _as expressed in the Anglo-Japanese Treaty of 1902_, January, the 30ᵗʰ, _and not to become a protectorate or a Confederation_ of any Power.

(2) The independence of the Corean Empire was _originally created by the initiative of Japan_, so I wish that this would be secured and maintained by her goodwill in the same manner as it created at the conclusion of the present hostility. Really the creation of the independence of one country by another is just like the plantation of a young tree by a gardener, and that the care and maintenance for its growth is encouraged by the law of Nature and good for the Means of History.

(3) As for the cause of the present hostility, it was chiefly due to the failure of the Russian evacuation of Manchuria, and there was very little question due to the Corean problems. Moreover, since the war broken out the actual area of the hostility is Manchuria and not Corea, and _in this sense_ that the independence and the integrity of the Corean Empire have no cause to be altered or impaired at the conclusion of the present hostility.

(4) Since the independence and the integrity of the Corean Empire be secured and maintained, it needs necessary privileges to maintain them, such as the _independent diplomatic and consular services_, the _independent army and police forces_, the _independent money_, the _independent posts and telegrams_, and the _independent customs_ &.

(5) However, in view of the recent alleged Russian Peace Terms with Japan, which was telegraphed by the

Reuters correspondent in St. Petersburg and was
published in all the London newspapers on the 22nd
ultimo, which was chiefly concerned to the independence
and the integrity of the Corean Empire _guaranteed_
by the Anglo-Japanese Treaty of 1902, January, the
80th, which I already brought to the notice of the British
Government on the 24th ultimo, and it was followed by
the alleged Japanese Peace Terms with Russia, which
was emanated from Washington on the 25th ultimo
and was also published in the London Evening newspapers on the same date.

(6) Happily these two alleged Peace Terms were denied as
devoid of foundation, but in view of the public opinion
current at present moment and of the existing character of the war in the Far East, this is the _matter of_
grave concern to the independence and the integrity
of the Corean Empire, therefore I beg to call the attention
of the British Government to _consider the Corean_
affairs according to Anglo-Japanese Treaty, and would
be so generous enough as to _make suggestions to both_
Russia and _Japan_ when the peace assured, and whatever may be the result of the war, to preserve the independence and the integrity of the Corean Empire. I
beg to express little further that it is the _ardent desire_
of His Majesty, the Emperor of Corea to see that a clause
be inserted in the Russo-Japanese Peace Treaty con....
the guarantee of the independence and the integrity of
the Corean Empire. Herewith I have the honour to
annex two pieces of newspapers which containing the
alleged Russian and Japanese Peace Terms for the
notice of the British Government.

1883-4-1   Blee.

Times.
February 22: 1905.

St James's Gazette.
February 25, 1905.

THE WAR.

(THE QUESTION OF PEACE.

OUTLINE OF THE RUSSIAN TERMS.

ST. PETERSBURG, Feb. 21.

In spite of official denials, information has reached Reuter's correspondent here from a source enjoying high patronage that not only has the question of peace been formally discussed by the Tsar, but that the conditions on which Russia is prepared to make peace have been practically agreed upon. These are as follows :—

(1) Korea to be placed under Japanese suzerainty, Port Arthur and the Liau-tung Peninsula to be ceded to Japan, Vladivostok to be declared a neutral port on the "open door" system, the Eastern Chinese Railway to be placed under a neutral international administration, and Manchuria as far north as Kharbin to be restored as an integral part of the Chinese Empire.

The difficulty lies in settling the question of the indemnity, which it is known that Japan insists on, but it is thought that the obstacle is not insuperable.

Although it is quite possible that Russia will risk another battle before a decision is arrived at, the most trustworthy opinion here is that, in view of the internal situation and the enormous difficulty of carrying on the war, peace on the terms outlined will be concluded, if the indemnity question can be arranged, within a comparatively short space of time.

On being shown the above telegram by a representative of Reuter's Agency, last evening, Viscount Hayashi, the Japanese Minister in London, stated that, while he regarded the statement contained in it as both interesting and important, he was far from being in a position to say what terms of peace would be acceptable to his Government. He had no information pointing to a speedy conclusion of hostilities. No overtures could come from the Japanese side. As to the probabilities of Russia's making overtures, he knew of no fresh factor except possibly the internal situation in that country, and that was still uncertain.

COLOGNE, Feb. 21.

In a Berlin telegram to the *Cologne Gazette* it is emphatically declared that the sole object of the journey of Prince Frederick Leopold of Prussia to St. Petersburg was that his Royal Highness might present himself to the Tsar before starting for the scene of war in Manchuria. There was no question of the Prince's being entrusted with a political mission, or even one directed towards mediation.

JAPANESE PEACE TERMS.

WOULD NOT HAGGLE OVER AN INDEM

NEW YORK.

A despatch from Washington says that Mr. Takahira, Japanese Minister, has submitted to President Roosevelt which Japan would be willing to make peace

According to Mr. Takahira's Note, Japan stipulates shall agree to—

(1) A complete and permanent evacuation of Manchuria an international guarantee that it shall remain an integral China.

(2) International management of the railroad from Port Arthur and Niuchwang.

(3) Recognition of Japan's influence in Korea.

(4) Japan's retention of Port Arthur, which would be the trade of all nations on an equal footing.

Mr. Takahira made no mention of any sum as an indemnity intimated that Japan would not haggle over the matter, no objection to Russia retaining Vladivostok.

Mr. Takahira did not ask that these terms should to Russia, but they have been cabled to Mr. McCormick Minister at St. Petersburg. Up to the present no reply received.— Central News.

COREA AND MANCHURIA. [March 6.]

CONFIDENTIAL. SECTION 1.

No. 1.

Corean Chargé d'Affaires to the Marquess of Lansdowne.—(Received March 6.) .

[Printed literally.]

My Lord, 4, *Trebovir Road, London, March 3*, 1905.

I HAVE the honour to inform your Lordship that I had took the opportunity of coming round to the Foreign Office on the 8th ultimo, and had a conversation with Mr. Langley on the subject of preserving the independence and the integrity of the Corean Empire, as expressed in the Anglo-Japanese Treaty of 1902, the 30th January, as Japan is so far successful in this present war.

I had intended to present a Memorandum to your Lordship for the above statement, but before that taken place there was the rumour of the alleged Russian peace terms with Japan which was emanating from St. Petersburgh, and was published in all the London newspapers on the 22nd ultimo, which was so seriously concerned to the independence and the integrity of the Corean Empire, guaranteed by the Anglo-Japanese Treaty of 1902, January the 30th. Therefore I addressed a note to Mr. Langley on the 24th ultimo concerning the said rumour, and further request him to take my statement, which I made to him on the 8th ultimo, as an official step ; and then there came another rumour from Washington on the 25th ultimo, concerning the alleged Japanese peace terms with Russia, which was so seriously concerned to the independence and the integrity of the Corean Empire as the alleged Russian peace terms.

This being the case, I dispatched a messenger to the Corean Government on the 24th ultimo concerning my statement made to Mr. Langley on the 8th ultimo and the alleged Russian peace terms with Japan ; and then another, on the 27th ultimo, concerning the alleged Japanese peace terms with Russia in the following sense : "So far as Japan is successful in this present war, and I believe that this will be the result of the end ; therefore it would be wise for the Corean Government to consider the question of preserving the independence and the integrity of the Corean Empire by means of Anglo-Japanese Treaty. This Treaty was concluded between Great Britain and Japan for the maintenance of the independence and the integrity of the Chinese and Corean Empires ; so I think it is advisable for the Corean Government to communicate with the British Government to render its support and preserve the independence and the integrity of the Corean Empire, according to Anglo-Japanese Treaty of 1902, January the 30th, and to further request to render the same support in the event of the Russian success. Great Britain is the only power to give weight in this matter." . P.S. "According to the alleged Russian peace terms with Japan, which was telegraphed from St. Petersburgh, and was published in all the London newspapers on the 22nd instant, the Article I expressing that 'Corea to be placed under Japanese suzerainty.' This Article is so seriously concerned to the independence and the integrity of the Corean Empire, guaranteed by the Anglo-Japanese Treaty of 1902, January the 30th, therefore I am communicating with the British Government concerning the said Russian peace terms. Instruct me to communicate further with the British Government."

I dispatched another message to the Corean Government on the 27th ultimo concerning the alleged Japanese peace terms with Russia, which was emanating from Washington, and was also published in the London evening newspapers on the 25th ultimo in the following sense : "According to the alleged Japanese peace terms with Russia, which was emanating from Washington, and was also published in the London evening newspapers on the 25th instant, the Article III expressing that "Russia shall recognize Japanese influence in Corea as supreme," and there no clause expressing the manner of guaranteeing the independence and the integrity of the Corean Empire. According to both Russian and Japanese peace terms, the matter is very serious for the independence and the integrity of the Corean Empire. Please instruct me to communicate with the British Government."

On the 28th ultimo I received the following telegram from my Government : " I approve your view on the situation. As for the attitude of the British Government towards the Corean affairs is most impressive from the beginning, and this is the fortune of the nation. As for the question of preserving the independence and the integrity of

[1883 *f*—1]

2

the Corean Empire, you come to understanding with the British Government so as to
insert in the coming Russo-Japanese peace Treaty an Article duly guaranteeing the
independence and the integrity of the Corean Empire." On receiving the above
instructions from my Government, herewith I have the honour to present to your
Lordship the accompanied Memorandum for the consideration of the British Government
towards the Corean affairs concerning the present situation.

I have, &c.

(Signed)   YI HAN EUNG.

Inclosure 1 in No. 1.

Memorandum.

SO far, Japan is successful in this present war, therefore I most earnestly wish
that the independence and the integrity of the Corean Empire would be secured and
maintained as expressed in the Anglo-Japanese Treaty of 1902, January, the 30th, and
not to become a Protectorate or a Confederation of any Power.

2. The independence of the Corean Empire was originally created by the initiative
of Japan, so I wish that this would be secured and maintained by her goodwill in the
same manner as it was created, at the conclusion of the present hostility. Really, the
creation of the independence of one country by another is just like the plantation of a
young tree by a gardener, and that the care and maintenance for its growth is encouraged
by the law of nature, and good for the means of history.

3. As for the cause of the present hostility, it was chiefly due to the failure of the
Russian evacuation of Manchuria, and there was very little question due to the Corean
problems. Moreover, since the war broken out, the actual area of the hostility is
Manchuria and not Corea, and in this sense that the independence and the integrity
of the Corean Empire have no cause to be altered or impaired at the conclusion of the
present hostility.

4. Since the independence and the integrity of the Corean Empire be secured and
maintained, it needs necessary privileges to maintain them, such as the independent
diplomatic and Consular services, the independent army and police forces, the
independent money, the independent posts and telegrams, and the independent
customs, &c.

5. However, in view of recent alleged Russian peace terms with Japan, which was
telegraphed by the Reuter's correspondent in St. Petersburgh, and was published in all
the London newspapers on the 22nd ultimo, which was chiefly concerned to the
independence and the integrity of the Corean Empire, guaranteed by the Anglo-
Japanese Treaty of 1902, January the 30th, which I already brought to the notice of
the British Government on the 24th ultimo, and it was followed by the alleged Japanese
peace terms with Russia, which was emanated from Washington on the 25th ultimo, and
was also published in the London evening newspapers on the same date.

6. Happily, these two alleged peace terms were denied as devoid of foundation,
but in view of the public opinion current at present moment, and of the existing
character of the war in the Far East, this is the matter of grave concern to the independence and the integrity of the Corean Empire, therefore, I beg to call the attention of
the British Government to consider the Corean affairs according to Anglo-Japanese
Treaty, and would be so generous enough to make suggestions to both Russia and
Japan when the peace assured, and whatever may be the result of the war, to preserve
the independence and the integrity of the Corean Empire. I beg to express little
further that it is the ardent desire of His Majesty the Emperor of Corea to see that a
clause be inserted in the Russo-Japanese Peace Treaty concerning the guarantee of the
independence and the integrity of the Corean Empire. Herewith I have the honour to
annex two pieces of newspapers which containing the alleged Russian and Japanese
peace terms for the notice of the British Government.

3

Inclosure 2 in No. 1.

Newspaper Extracts.

(1.)

The " Times " of February 22, 1905.

THE QUESTION OF PEACE.

OUTLINE OF THE RUSSIAN TERMS.

IN spite of official denials, information has reached Reuter's correspondent here from a source enjoying high patronage that not only has the question of peace been formally discussed by the Czar, but that the conditions on which Russia is prepared to make peace have been practically agreed upon. ' These are as follows :—

1. Corea to be placed under Japanese suzerainty ;
2. Port Arthur and the Liau-tung Peninsula to be ceded to Japan ;
3. Vladivostock to be declared a neutral port on the " open-door " system ;
4. The Eastern Chinese Railway to be placed under a neutral international administration ; and
5. Manchuria as far north as Harbin to be restored as an integral part of the Chinese Empire.

The difficulty lies in settling the question of the indemnity, which it is known that Japan insists on, but it is thought that the obstacle is not insuperable.

Although it is quite possible that Russia will risk another battle before a decision is arrived at, the most trustworthy opinion here is that, in view of the internal situation and the enormous difficulty of carrying on the war, peace on the terms outlined will be concluded, if the indemnity question can be arranged, within a comparatively short space of time.

On being shown the above telegram by a representative of Reuter's Agency, last evening, Viscount Hayashi, the Japanese Minister in London, stated that, while he regarded the statement contained in it as both interesting and important, he was far from being in a position to say what terms of peace would be acceptable to his Government. He had no information pointing to a speedy conclusion of hostilities. No overtures could come from the Japanese side. As to the probabilities of Russia's making overtures, he knew of no fresh factor except possibly the internal situation in that country, and that was still uncertain.

St. Petersburgh, February 21, 1905.

In a Berlin telegram to the " Cologne Gazette " it is emphatically declared that the sole object of the journey of Prince Frederick Leopold of Prussia to St. Petersburgh was that his Royal Highness might present himself to the Czar before starting for the scene of war in Manchuria. There was no question of the Prince's being intrusted with a political Mission, or even one directed towards mediation.

Cologne, February 21, 1905.

(5)

The "St. James' Gazette" of February 25, 1905.

JAPANESE PEACE TERMS.

WOULD NOT HAGGLE OVER AN INDEMNITY.

A despatch from Washington says that Mr. Takahira, the Japanese Minister, has submitted to President Roosevelt the terms on which Japan would be willing to make peace.

According to Mr. Takahira's note, Japan stipulates that Russia shall agree to—

1. A complete and permanent evacuation of Manchuria, and to an international guarantee that it shall remain an integral part of China;

2. International management of the railroad from Harbin to Port Arthur and Newchwang;

3. Recognition of Japan's influence in Corea as supreme;

4. Japan's retention of Port Arthur, which would be open to the trade of all nations on an equal footing.

Mr. Takahira made no mention of any sum as an indemnity, and intimated that Japan would not haggle over the matter. There was no objection to Russia retaining Vladivostock.

Mr. Takahira did not ask that these terms should be submitted to Russia, but they have been cabled to Mr. McCormick, American Minister at St. Petersburgh. Up to the present no reply has been received.

New York, Saturday.

Dft.

Yi Han Eung

F.O.

March 13 1905

Sir,

I have the honour

to ack. the receipt of

your Note of the 3rd

instant, relative to the

position of Corea after

the Conclusion of the

war between Russia

and Japan

While thanking you for your

Communication, ~~in reply~~ I have

the honour to state

that ay discussion of

the ~~terms of peace~~

Print (Corea & Manchuria)
Peking
Tokio

affecting Corea would
not, in my opinion,
be likely to have any
useful results at the
present moment

4. Trebovir Road,
Earls Court.
London, S.W. March 22, 1905.

His Lordship,
The Most Hon. the Marquess of Lansdowne, K. G.
The Principal Secretary of State for Foreign Affairs.

My Lord,
I have the honour to inform your Lordship that I had communicated with the Corean Government your Lordship's reply of the 13th instant to my note of the 3rd, and I received the following instructions from my Government on the 20th instant to communicate further with the British Government :-

"You express the sincere thanks of the Corean Government for the kind sentiment of the British Government, and at the same time you request the British Government to be so good enough as to consider the Corean affairs according to Anglo-Japanese Treaty, and whatever may be the result of the present war, to make suggestions to both Russia and Japan whenever there is a prospect of peace to insert in the coming Russo-Japanese Peace Treaty a clause duly guaranteeing the independence and the territorial integrity of the Corean Empire."

2 - 1883 aar

In bringing to the notice of your lordship the
above instructions I beg to add my cordial thanks,
and I most earnestly wish that the British
Government would be so generous enough as to
render its kind efforts for the said affairs when
the right time comes.

> I have the honour to be,
> With highest consideration,
>> Sir,
>> your lordship's most obedient,
>>> humble servant,
>>> Yi Han Eung

Q $\frac{22}{24}$? March 1905.

(Ref. FO. Mch. 13)

Position of Corea after the war.

Corean Govt. request H.M.G. to suggest
to Russia & Japan inserting. in Peace
Treaty. clause guaranteeing independence
& integrity of Corea.

Print (Corea & Manchuria) 3/4
Seoul

Q? Ack. receipt.

Dft
Lrd.
April: 1. 05   L.

72 Corea

[This Document is the Property of His Britannic Majesty's Government.]

COREA AND MANCHURIA.   [March 24.]

CONFIDENTIAL.   Section 2.

No. 1.

Yi Han Eung to the Marquess of Lansdowne.—(Received March 24.)

My Lord,   *Corean Legation, London, March 22, 1905.*

I HAVE the honour to inform your Lordship that I had communicated with the Corean Government your Lordship's reply of the 13th instant to my note of the 3rd, and I received the following instructions from my Government on the 20th instant to communicate further with the British Government :—

"You express the sincere thanks of the Corean Government for the kind sentiment of the British Government, and at the same time you request the British Government to be so good enough as to consider the Corean affairs according to Anglo-Japanese Treaty, and whatever may be the result of the present war, to make suggestions to both Russia and Japan whenever there is a prospect of peace to insert in the coming Russo-Japanese Peace Treaty a clause duly guaranteeing the independence and the territorial integrity of the Corean Empire."

In bringing to the notice of your Lordship the above instructions I beg to add my cordial thanks, and I most earnestly wish that the British Government would be so generous enough as to render its kind efforts for the said affairs when the right time comes.

I have, &c.
(Signed)   YI HAN EUNG.

[1883 aa—2]

F.O.
April 1. 05

Draft
ji Han. ung

unt (Corea & manchuria)
Seoul.

Sir,

I have the honour
to acknowledge the receipt
of your note of the 22nd
ult relative to the position
of Corea after the conclusion
of the war between Russia
and Japan

I have the honour to
express my thanks for
your communication.

Draft

Yi Han Eung

F.O April 1. 1905.

(Ref his Mch 22)

Position of Corea after war

Acks his letter

Print (Corea + Manchuria)

Seoul

COREA AND MANCHURIA.   [April 1.]

CONFIDENTIAL.   SECTION 3.

No. 1.

The Marquess of Lansdowne to Yi Han Eung.

Sir,   *Foreign Office, April 1, 1905.*
    I HAVE the honour to acknowledge the receipt of your note of the 22nd ultimo relative to the position of Corea after the conclusion of the war between Russia and Japan.

                              I have, &c.
                    (Signed)   LANSDOWNE.

[1934 a—3]

4, Trebovir Road,
Earls Court,
London, S.W. April 8, 1905.

His Lordship,
The Most Hon. the Marquess of Lansdowne, K.G.
The Principal Secretary of State for Foreign Affairs.

My Lord,

I have the honour to inform your Lordship that I had lost no time in communicating with the Corean Government your Lordship's reply of the 1st instant to my note of the 22nd ultimo, and I beg to express my earnest wish that my previous two notes will receive generous consideration of the British Government when the war concludes between Russia and Japan.

I have the honour to be,
with highest consideration,
Sir,
your Lordship's most obedient,
humble servant,
Yi Han Eung.

Yi Han bung

⊕ 8/11 } April 1905.
　(Ref. F.O. Apr. 1)

Position of Corea after the war
Hopes his previous notes will receive
glorious consider- at end of war.

This is practically
an acknowledgment of
our note and requires
no answer.
　　　　　　　　 4z.
　　　　　F.C.

100. Corea.

4, Trebovir Road,
Earls Court,
London, S.W. April 17. 1905.

Sir,

I have the honour to inform you that I myself being the Representative of a friendly Nation at this Court, so I think it is quite obligatory for me to call the attention of this Britannic Majesty's Government to avert my personal danger if there is such a circumstance.

On the 12th instant I went out for a walk to Hyde Park and I stood by the serpentine about 3.30. p.m. and taking air, then two men came, one sat on the bench aside and the other stood by the former and they spoke with each other, but which I could not hear distinctly, and they looked somewhat like foreigners.

The man stood by the bench spoke something to the other sat on the bench, then the latter made some hint to the former and it probably was to do some thing to me. Then the man coming to me and I found that he was so disagreeable and I left that spot immediately.

Then the man spoke very emphatically that "he is lucky, very clever, very clever", and according to the terms used by him that he had an intention of making attempt upon my life.

This being the case, herewith I have the honour of calling the attention of His Britannic Majesty's Government to take adequate measure and to secure my personal safety whenever I am going out on business or on walk while I am at this Court, which I will esteem as a greatest favour in this world, and I won't forget it a the times. Awaiting your early and favourable reply.

I have the honour to be,
with highest consideration,
Sir,
Your most obedient,
humble servant.
Yi Han Eung.

F. A. Campbell Esq.

R 178 } April 1905.

<u>His personal safety</u>
Requests measures to ensure:
Relates suspicious incident in
Hyde Park.

I suppose that we
must send this letter
to the Home Office for
aber
such action as they
practicable
may consider advisable
Ers. And inform.
But it is ridiculous A.R.

JaC

Dfts { Yi Han Eung
Home Office
April 22 1905

102 Corea

Scott.

Dft.

I Han Eung
4 Trebovir Road
Earls Court.
S.W.

F.O.
April 22 1905.

Sir,

I have the
honour to ack. the
receipt of your
letter of the 17th
inst relating the
circles which lead
you to believe that
your personal safety
in London is endangered
and asking that the
necessary measures

may be taken for
Your protection.

In reply I have
the honour to inform
You that a commun.
in the sense desired
by you has been
~~addressed to the~~
S of S for the Home
Department.

Fat.

[to Home Office
April 22 1905]

4, Trebovir Road,
Earls Court,
London, S.W. April 29, 1905.

His Lordship,
The Most Hon: the Marquess of Lansdowne, K.G.
The Principal Secretary of State for Foreign Affairs.

My Lord, I have the honour to acknowledge the receipt of your Lordship's reply of the 22nd instant to my note of the 17th addressed to Mr. Campbell, your Lordship's Assistant Under-Secretary of State, and I beg to express my profound thanks and gratitude for the kindness of His Britannic Majesty's Government as to take necessary measures in order to secure my personal safety against possible danger.

In the mean while, I have the honour to express my regret for my troublesome request made to His Britannic Majesty's Government for my personal safety through an unfortunate incident while I am in such a gracious Court as this, and I beg to express further my wish that I hope to use all my efforts and to promote Anglo-Corean interests in the long run as well as possible.

I have the honour to be
with highest consideration,

Yi Han Tang

D 29 April 1905.
R 1 May

(Rf ?0 Apl 22)

His personal safety
Thanks for measures taken.

We told him that
a Comm.? had been
addressed to the Home
Secretary about his
personal Safety He
is Satisfied and even
gratified [Badly folded]

The Japanese Minister
told us [before received]
110. Corea.

Neighbours of Yi Han
Sung who thought
that he was with

JHB

27

4. Trebovir Road,
Earls Court,
London, S.W. — May 11. 1905.

My Dear Sir,

I have duly received your kind note of yesterday's date, and I must earnestly wish you to be so good enough as to convey my most profound thanks for the kind inquiries and wishes of his lordship, the most Hon. the Marquess of Lansdowne, K.G. for my recent illness and its speedy recovery.

I have further, to inform you that I have some important matter to convey in an interview which is graciously proposed to be granted by his lordship, the Most Hon. the Marquess of Lansdowne, K.G. in his lordship's convenient time, which are equally concerns to my country and my person.

At the same time I will firmly follow the recommendation of my medical advice, and I beg to express my sincere thanks for your kind wishes.

I have the honour to be with highest consideration

Sir,
Your most obedient,
humble servant,

Dft.
Home Office

F.O.

April 22 1905.

Yi Han Eung
April 17. 1905

Sir,

I am directed
by the Marquess of
Lansdowne to tr: to
you, for such action
as the S. of S. for the
Home Dept. may
consider practicable
and advisable, a
copy of a letter which
has been received
from the Corean Ch:
d'Aff. at this Court

Stating that he
considers his personal
Safety in London is
endangered and
asking that measures
may be taken to.
protect him.

R ⅔ } May 1ᵗʰ 1905.
(Ref FO. Apl 22)

Personal safety of Corean Ch. d' Aff.
He is suffering from melancholia &
mental depression. Police will
endeavour to reassure him

Mr. Yi Han Eung has
already been informed
that we were in
communication with the
Home Office and has
Expressed his thanks.
    No further commⁿ to
him would appear to be
necessary. He has gone
III. Corea. to Brighton, I believe
                            JAE

(2)

...in some other way, and I beg to assume that it will be a great measure in the future (and even at present) for the two governments to come to thorough understanding and our mutual interests will be best secured in this way,

(1) To protect the Independence, sovereignty, and integrity of Corea according to the feature of Anglo-Japanese Treaty.

(2) To prevent any aggression power from taking the control of Corean Government in any respects.

(3) To prevent any aggressive [...] from bringing troops into Corean interior without any serious disturbance which threaten the lives and properties of foreigners therein.

(4) If there be any disturbance or riot, [...] must bear first and full duty to [...] order in consequence of its sovereignty.

(5) In case there to be Russo Japanese War the British Government will render its efforts to preserve the Independence, sover[...]

(1)

2

integrity and the privileges of Corea, as they are now by some to understanding with different powers, on whichever side the history may be derived.

January, 13. 1904

(1)

Great Britain.   Russia.

Anglo   Russian string.

France   Japanese string.

France.   Japan.

The world politics is just like a sort of machine as showing in this diagram, and if these two ends of the balance in the Far East try to go forward to collapse with each other, then naturally the other two in the Eastern West will be wide opened, and in other sense, they have reciprocal motion and will collapse in both ends.

If this being the case, China and Corea will be pressed and crushed in the Far East and Great Britain and France will collapse with each other on this side, and perhaps there is a third power in Europe will avail herself to derive her fuller advantages and another third power in the Far East, but of which I cannot tell.

Therefore Great Britain and France must come to understanding with each other in order to press

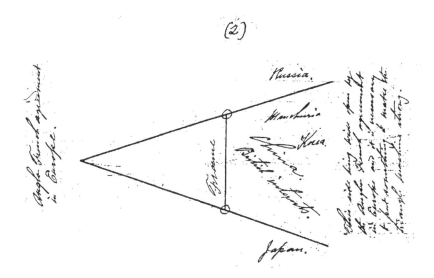

If Great Britain and France come to an
agreement on this side of Europe, then the position
of the world politics will be the same as showing
in this diagram, that the two ends of the balance
in Europe will be combined together by Anglo-French
agreement and the other two in the Far East will
be wide opened, and then China and Korea will be
saved; British position in the Far East will be strength-
tened, and the third powers both in Europe and
the Far East could not try to seek for their political
advantages.

It is an obvious advantages for France to
come to an understanding with Great Britain as
they are first rate powers in this present world, and
the French position both in Europe and the Far

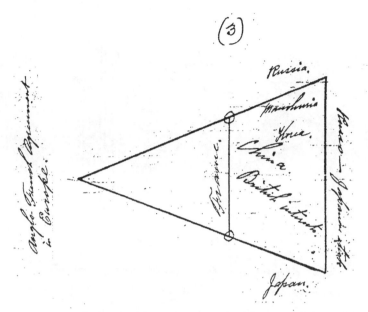

At present the two ends of the political balance in the Far East being wide opened by the agreement of Great Britain and France on this side of Europe, and they try to put a stick or bar between to maintain the balance but the Russo-Japanese stick is a joint and not natural and durable.

It will always be in disorder and variance and will always be shaken by their constant motion, and the middle parts of the balance shall be broken in spite of Anglo-French agreement on this side of Europe.

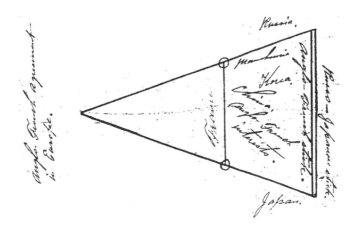

As showing in the previous diagram that the Russo-Japanese stick is not natural and smooth, but only a joint one for the moment, and it wont maintain the political balance as far as possible and therefore it would be much better to put an anglo French stick inside the Russo-Japanese one, then the political machine would be strong enough as long as the Anglo French stick is there, and this can be done by Great Britain and France acting as umpires to settle the Russo Japanese dispute and guarantee their mutual interests in Manchuria and Korea, which has always been the question and does not come to an agreement on the ground of their mutual suspicion being attacked or injured by either in the future.

It is very necessary for Great Britain and

Great Britain.   Russia.

The World of peace, prosperity,
civilization, and Commerce
etc.

France.   Japan.

they bound to share common interests and common
danger.

If there will be a treaty of four powers
alliance) for the Far Eastern affairs, then it is
advisable for Great Britain and France to be
their alliances as far as possible.

I do not think that the Anglo-Japan
and Franco-Russian alliances are the dead
ones, and I think it is high time for Great
Britain and France to create a treaty of four
powers for the Far Eastern affairs as well as
for the worlds.

If this could be done, then such an unheard
deed would be formed for the first time in the
history as the two similar allies formed a peace
party instead of war, and secure the peace
of the world.

As for the Corean affairs, I pledge the
unhappy Far Eastern Peninsula to the British
Government and I hope that its sovereignty,
integrity and privileges are not to be injured
or impaired in the long run.

I have availed myself of giving round to
the Foreign office on few occasions and expressed
my absurd opinions, but I kept them quite
robust and same in the future.

My only desire is to create a splendid
chapter in the British and World History under
the title of "Lord Lansdowne's Far Eastern policy"
and to lessen the deep melancholy and
sorrow of the poor Corean Emperor and his
subjects.

In case of my opinion is against the
British foreign policy in any respects, I wish
the Foreign office would be so kind enough
as to take it as my personal mistake and
not an official one.

I beg to further assure that, by the geographical point of view, the Corean Peninsula
is the Key-stone of the political arch in the
Far East, the powerful left arm of Russian
giant and the bridge of Japan to the Asiatic
Continent, so I think it is the policy of the
greatest world power to keep it as far as
possible.

Corean Ch. d'Aff. Jan 13/04

Foreign Office.

9

This seems to be virtually a request for a British guarantee of Korea against Japan as well as Russia.

We cannot open discussions upon such a proposal.

It would be suff. to tell the Ch. d'Aff. that her policy may be gathered from the ... statement ...

at a moment like the
present to supplement that agreement
by a further understanding
just as he apparently
desires

L 19/1
Draft
Ain : :04.

The Corea Chargé d'Af:
Called this afternoon
& left the enclosed Mem.
which however contains
no more than that he
communicated on the 13th

I told him, in
accordance with Lord
Lansdowne's instructions
that as was apparent
from the Anglo-Japanese

that it was out of the
question that HMGov't
should give Corea
a guarantee to that
effect. He said he
"had been informed
by telegraph from Seoul
that Japanese soldiers
disguised as "merchants"
were being introduced
into the interior of Corea.
He could not say any-
thing as regards Russia"

He further stated that
the Corean Gov't would
not give to either the
Russians or Coreans [Japs?]
a concession for the
construction of the
Seoul - Wiju Railway,
as the Corean Gov't
desired to build it
themselves. For this
purpose the Corean
Gov't desired to obtain
a loan from the British
Gov't. I said the British
Gov't

With Corean min' Jan 20/04.

Gov't did not lend
money to foreign gov'ts
for building railways,
and that the Corean
Gov't had better not
count on obtaining any
assistance in the matter
from this country.

Feb Jan 19. 04

L

*Agreement between Great Britain and Japan, signed at London,
January 30. 1902.*

THE Governments of Great Britain and Japan, actuated solely by a desire to maintain the *status quo* and general peace in the extreme East, being moreover specially interested in maintaining the independence and territorial integrity of the Empire of China and the Empire of Corea, and in securing equal opportunities in those countries for the commerce and industry of all nations, hereby agree as follows :—

ARTICLE I.

The High Contracting Parties having mutually recognized the independence of China and of Corea, declare themselves to be entirely uninfluenced by any aggressive tendencies in either country. Having in view, however, their special interests, of which those of Great Britain relate principally to China, while Japan, in addition to the interests which she possesses in China, is interested in a peculiar degree politically, as well as commercially and industrially, in Corea, the High Contracting Parties recognize that it will be admissible for either of them to take such measures as may be indispensable in order to safeguard those interests if threatened either by the aggressive action of any other Power, or by disturbances arising in China or Corea, and necessitating the intervention of either of the High Contracting Parties for the protection of the lives and property of its subjects.

ARTICLE II.

If either Great Britain or Japan, in the defence of their respective interests as above described, should become involved in war with another Power, the other High Contracting Party will maintain a strict neutrality, and use its efforts to prevent other Powers from joining in hostilities against its ally.

ARTICLE III.

If in the above event any other Power or Powers should join in hostilities against that ally, the other High Contracting Party will come to its assistance and will conduct the war in common, and make peace in mutual agreement with it.

ARTICLE IV.

The High Contracting Parties agree that ——————— consulting the other, enter into separate arrangements with another Power to the prejudice of the interests above described.

ARTICLE V.

Whenever, in the opinion of either Great Britain or Japan, the above-mentioned interests are in jeopardy, the two Governments will communicate with one another fully and frankly.
[239]

The present Agreement shall come into effect immediately after the date of its signature, and remain in force for five years from that date.

In case neither of the High Contracting Parties should have notified twelve months before the expiration of the said five years the intention of terminating it, it shall remain binding until the expiration of one year from the day on which either of the High Contracting Parties shall have denounced it. But if, when the date fixed for its expiration arrives, either ally is actually engaged in war, the alliance shall, *ipso facto*, continue until peace is concluded.

In faith whereof the Undersigned, duly authorized by their respective Governments, have signed this Agreement, and have affixed thereto their seals.

Done in duplicate at London, the 30th January, 1902.

(L.S.)   (Signed)   LANSDOWNE,
His Britannic Majesty's Principal
Secretary of State for Foreign
Affairs.

(L.S.)   (Signed)   HAYASHI,
Envoy Extraordinary and Minister
Plenipotentiary of His Majesty
the Emperor of Japan at the
Court of St. James.

(40.)

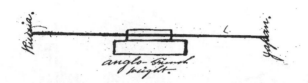

Now Great Britain and France became the weight of the Russo-Japanese balance in the Far East and that they can preserve its equibilium as far as possible, as they can move their weight on this side or the other as the balance moves.

It is the policy of Great Britain and France to preserve the existing condition of the present world, policy of Japan and Russia to fight at their risks, policy of China and Corea to be protected, and the policy of two third powers both in the war and the want to urge the Russo-Japanese war, and at the same time Great Britain and France will naturally be involved in the same.

January 19. 1904.

(4b.)

In my previous diagram I suggested
to put an anglo French stick inside the
Russo-Japanese joint one in order to maintain
the political machine in the Far East as
far as possible, and to avoid the variance
and discord of the Russo-Japanese joint
stick, which will cause the fraction of the
middle part of the balances in the near future.
   Great Britain and France can do double
functions in this present world, since they
have come to an agreement in the west,
that they can move few steps eastwards and
put a cross stick between the anglo-Japanese
and Franco-Russian sticks and put nails
on, then the political machine in the Far
East would be as strong as possible, and at
the same time there must be two other sticks
up and below between the anglo-Russian and
Franco-Japanese sticks.
   I should be very glad to learn that
Lord Lansdowne signed this treaty.

Jannary 19. 1904.

I have received a telegraphic instruction from His Majesty, the Emperor of Corea, my sovereign to communicate with His Britannic Majesty's Government to give a push note and guarantee that the Corean Government will not be interfered by any aggressive power in any respect at present moment as well as in the future; and in the event of Russo-Japanese breaking out in the Far East, Great Britain will come to understanding with different powers before or on the outbreak of the said war and guarantee that the independence, integrity, sovereignty, and the privileges will not be impaired in any way, on whichever side the victory may be decided, and further ask the favour of the British Government to prevent any aggressive power from bringing troops into Corean interior without any serious disturbance which threatens the lives of and properties of foreigners therein, and whenever there is a disturbance in Corea the Corean Government must have first and full city to restore order in connection of arising.

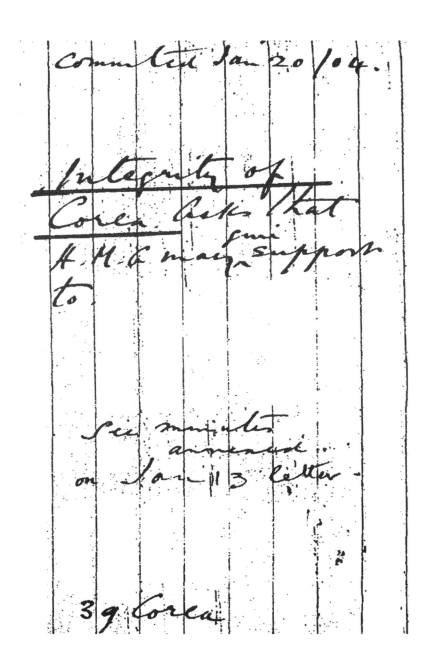

4. Trebovir Road,
Earls Court,
London, s.w. January 2.2. 190:

His Lordship,
The Most Hon. the Marquees of Lansdowne, K.G.
The Principal Secretary of State for Freign Affair

My Lord,
I have the honour to inform your lordsh
that I have just received a telegraphic instruction
from my Government to communicate with His
Britannic Majesty's Government the following declara

"Vu les complications que ont surgés entre
Russie et le Japone et au les difficultés que semble
rencontrer les negotiateurs a amener une solutio
pacifique le gouvernement Coréen par ordre de e
Majesté l'empereur declare qu'il a pris la ferm
resolution d'observer la plus stricte neutralité qu
que soit le resultat les pourparler actuellemen
engages entre les dites puissances, et Sa Majess
l'empereur compte en cette occasion sur le concou
amical de toutes les puissances."

I have the honour to be,
with highest consideration,
sir,

Draft

Yi Han Eung.

Copy to Admirty
with Yi Han Eung.
April: 19.

F. O.

April. 23 . 1904.

. Sir,

I have the honour
to acknowledge the
receipt of your note
of the 19th instant in
which you convey the
thanks of H.M. the Emperor
of Corea for the services
rendered by British
harmies in extinguishing
the recent fire at
the Imperial Palace at
Soul.

I have the honour

t.

Brooke

F.O.

Jan. 4ᵗʰ   1904

Dft.
igence Div

ersing

The Under Secretary
of State presents his
compliments to the
Director of Military
Intelligence & is directed
by the Marquess of
Lansdowne to inform
him that on Dec. 19ᵗʰ
the Commander in-Chief
on the China Station
telegraphed to H.M.
Minister at Seoul
asking his views as to
the probability of its
being necessary to
send a ship to Chemulpo

in view of possibilities.
Mr Jordan replied
that the presence of a
ship would be extremely
desirable, & that, if
possible, she should bring
a guard of twenty
men for the protection
of the Legation. He
added that there were
9000 native soldiers in
Seoul under very loose
control.

The Admiral telegraphed
on the 21st inst that

that she would embark
a Captain & twenty
marines of H.M.S.
"Cressy" which was
then at Wei-hai-wei.
Orders had been given
for a guard only to be
landed on a written
requisition from
H.M. Minister.

H.M.S "Sirius" arrived
at Chemulpo on the
27th ultimo

On the 29th Dec. the
Admiralty communicated

& that the guard would
probably not be required
unless there were war.
It was added that
Capt. Jones, R. M. had
been ordered to
report on the defence
of the Legation & the safety
of British subjects in
Seoul & Chemulpo.

A telegram, of which
a copy is inclosed,
has been received
from H.M. Minister
at Seoul, stating that
a U.S. transport
will arrive at Chemulpo
today, & that the

U.S. Minister proposes
to land at once thirty
men.

Mr Jordan considers
that it might be
advisable, as a precautionary
measure, to land a good
the
of twenty men from
H.M.S. "Sirius" for the
protection of the Legation
& states that, if approved, he would
act simultaneously
with the U.S. Minister.

Lord Lansdowne
would be glad to be
furnished with Sir
William Nicholson's
observations on the
enclosed

enclosed tel., & with
his opinion, as to
whether, should the
native troops' & the
population of Seoul
get beyond control,
a guard of twenty
men. will be sufficient.

On the last
occasion, in Dec. 1898,
when it was considered
necessary to land
men for the protection
of H.M. Legation at
Seoul, it was found
that there was only
accommodation available
for

for sixteen men.
At that time H.m.
Minister expressed the
opinion that the Legation
could not be adequately
protected with a
guard of less than
that number.

FH l

F.O. Jan 4. 1904

Situation at Seoul
Reports asks opinion
Concerning. for Mr
Jordan let no 2 of Jan 2

3 Corea

INTELLIGENCE DIVISION,
WINCHESTER HOUSE,
ST. JAMES'S SQUARE,
S.W.

5th January, 1904.

he Director General of Mobilization and Military Intelligence
ts his compliments to the Under Secretary of State for
n Affairs, and with reference to his letter of the 4th instant,
ing a copy of Mr. Jordan's telegram No. 2 of the 2nd instant,
o submit the following observations with respect to the
tion of His Majesty's Legation at Seoul :-
here appears to be every probability of energetic action
taken by Japan, should the answer by Russia to her latest
als be couched in such terms as to preclude all probability
cessful issue to the negotiations. Such action might take
rm of an occupation of part of Korea.
f it is held that such action on the part of Japan would
er the safety of His Majesty's Legation and of British
ts in Seoul, and in this connection the opinion of Mr Jordan
e held to carry weight, it appears obvious that a British
should be at hand in case of emergency, and the opportunity
ding a British force simultaneously with a United States'
force

force would probably produce a good effect as shewing unity of purpose.

The Guard of 20 men asked for by Mr Jordan might be sufficie to secure the safety of the Legation for a short time, but would clearly be an inadequate force to hold its own in Seoul against any serious attack, which might be made in overwhelming numbers. If, therefore, the situation is considered by Mr Jordan to be likely to become dangerous, there appear to be two courses open, viz.

(a) To send to Seoul at once a force of at least similar strength to that which the United States propose to land viz. 100 men.

(b) To send to Seoul the small guard of 20 men proposed by Mr Jordan and to hold in readiness at Chemulpo, i.e., at a distance of 26 miles by rail or road, the remainder of the 100 men.

Owing to the probable difficulty of obtaining quarters, (b) might be the better course to adopt. In either case there would 100 British troops at or near Seoul, which with the 100 men of the United States and the two companies of Japanese troops in Seoul - say 300 men - would make a total force of 500 men.

The

case of disturbance, the Japanese and United States troops
would co-operate in the protection of the British Legation and in
the maintenance of order.

R Jan 5. 1904
[ref ZO of Jan 4]

Defence of Seoul
Legation. Thinks it
desirable to send 100
men to Chemulpo, of which
at least 20 should proceed
at once to Seoul

Q[?] Authorize landing
of 20 men and ask if[?]
proper short arrangements
could be made at Seoul
or Chemulpo for
accommodation of further
force. We know that
of Corea the

Legation is very limited

Dfo[?]. Tel. annexed

R.

I think we must
tel. as proposed
before saying
anything to Admlty
as to an additional
force. It may not
be possible to
accommodate them.

Tal

L

" Tel sent Jan 6

F. O.

January 8 1902

Draft

Admiralty

" & Confidential

from Mr Jordan No 2/04
to Mr Jordan No 1/04
from Mr Jordan No 9/04

Sir,

I in

your letter, marked M
confidential, of the 21st
all ~~enclosing~~ a copy of
a telegram from the
Commander - in - Chief,
China, was ~~inclosed~~,
stating that orders had
been given for a guard
to be landed from H.M.S.
"Sirius" for the protection

of

of H. M. Legation at Seoul ~~to that effect was received from~~

~~on the~~ requisition of H. M.

Minister at that Capital.

I am directed by

The Marquess of Lansdowne

to transmit to You a

copy of a telegram from

Mr. Jordan reporting

that a guard ~~might~~ would

be landed ~~from~~ for the

protection of the U. S.

Legation, and that it

would be advisable as

a precautionary measure

to land a guard of

20 men for the protection

of

H.B.M. Legation.

Mr. Jordan proposed therefore to act simultaneously with the U.S. Minister in the matter.

The Direction of Mobiliz[n] & Military Intelligence who was consulted with regard to Mr. Jordan's proposal, expressed the opinion that if the situation were likely to become dangerous, a guard of 20 men should be sent to Seoul at once, and an additional 80 men held in readiness at Chemulpo.

A telegram was

Stevenson

thereupon addressed to
Mr. Jordan enquiring whether
20 men would be a
sufficient protection for
the Legation, ~~and~~ in the
Event of hostilities, and
what arrangements
could be made either at
Soul or Chemulpo for the
~~accommodation~~ of a portion
~~force~~

A telegram has now
been received from Mr.
Jordan stating that he has
informed the Commander-in-
Chief that one ship will
be ~~enough~~ sufficient at
Chemulpo

Chemulpo provided. She
can supply men to
reinforce the Legation guard
if necessary.

Mr. Jordan adds that
twenty men were to be
landed today

I am to inclose, for
the information of the
Lords Commis. of the
Admiralty, copies of the
papers referred to, and
I am to inquire whether
a reinforcement for the
Legation guard can be
held in readiness
at Chemulpo for despatch
to Seoul in case of necessity.

J.a.C

Admiralty

Immediate & Confidential

F.O. Jan. 8- 1904
3 Inclo.
[Their of Dec. 21/03]

Legation guard at Seoul

tr. Mr Jordan's tel. nos
2 & 9 of Jan. 2 and 7
& tel. to him no. 1 of
Jan. 6.
Informs of opinion of
Director Gen. of Mil. Int.
& asks if a reinforcement
can be kept ready at
Chemulpo.

7 Corea

BELMONT,
    DENMARK VILLAS,
      HOVE.

January 8th 1904.

The Most Noble the Marquis
of Lansdowne.

My Lord,

    May I venture to engage
and draw your Lordship's attention to a
new pledge that Russia enters into
with the English Government in 1887,
that if she retired from Port Hamilton,
she is convinced the Korean (Channel
that she (Russia) would not encroach
on Corean territory.
the present serious misunderstanding
with Japan, verging on War is connected

49

with her departure attitude to the Powers again to Sir Charles Dilke...the day in general with regard to Manchuria. Under Secretary repeats the statement and her distinct breach of promises with England regarding Corea, are clear. Parliamentary Paper (China No. 1 of 1885) has been repeatedly referred to in the House of Commons during both the Conservative and Liberal Governments. If Sir E. Ashmead Bartlett asked a question in 1895, and Sir Edward Grey replied that "in the event of the British occupation of Port Hamilton ceasing enable England to protect and interfere or her own rights without any way affecting the latest action taken by the above mentioned Powers in connection with Port Arthur, which was held in 1860 and honorably given up.

[illegible]

[illegible]

[illegible] to be

[illegible] Superintendent of Police

[illegible] Alipore in the 24 Pergunnahs

[illegible] your Lordship [illegible] illegally

[illegible] the privileges of [illegible]

[illegible] your [illegible].

I have the honour to be

My Lord [illegible]

Your obedient [illegible]

H. K. Banerjee.

Mr H. W. Bamber

D 8
R 13 January 1904

Russia & Corea :—

Calls attention to Russia's
Pledge of 1887 enabling England
to interfere on her own rights

Draft.
Jan. 20: 04   Ack d. — with thanks.

The ~~~~ give at
the time Port Hamilton was
~~evacuated~~ ~~~~ was locked up
the ~~~ day.   42

31. Corea   746

Bay View.
Chefoo.
China
9th January 1904

My Lord

I have the honour
to forward by this mail
under separate registered
cover copy of a Chart
of the Yalu which I made
last autumn. My work
was just finished when
the ice closed in, on 21
November.

This region having
come into special prominence
thing in deed under the

focus of all eyes out here,
it occurs to me that my
chart of this unsurveyed
district
~~...~~ may be of use
for reference, in view of
possible future events.

I may add that I
have sent copies to the
Naval Commander in Chief
and Sir Ernest Satow, to
whom, as well as my
Consular Officers, I have
endeavoured to give
all the information I
possess upon the Yalu
question.

I have verified my

work by piloting two steamers
to Sha ho, or Antung, and
now that I have found
the leading marks whereby
the river can be safely
entered from the East, I
believe a large steamer
traffic will spring upon on
this waterway.

I have the honour, to be
Your Lordship's Obedient
Servant
Mortimer O'Sullivan Capt.

The Right Honble
The Secretary of State for Foreign Affairs
Foreign Office
London S.W.

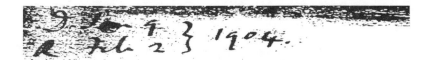

9 Jan
R Feb 2 } 1904.

Chart of the Yalu.
Is forwarding under
separate cover.

Ackd. with thanks
and send copy of letter
and Chart to Admiralty.
P.L. 4623

56 Corea

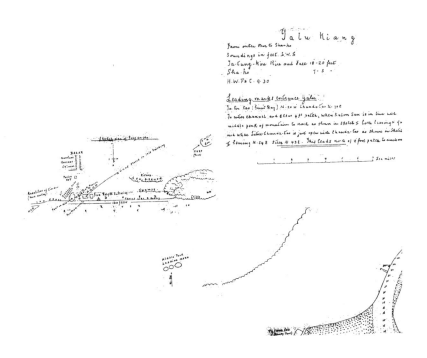

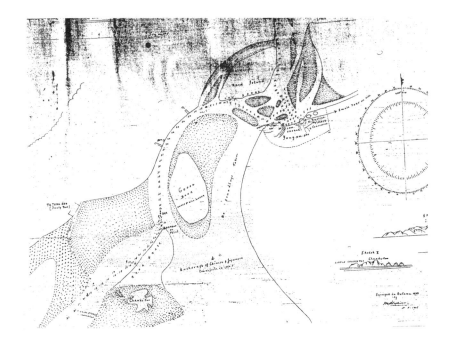

Enclosure,
in Capt: O'Sullivan
~~with~~　Jan. 9 - 1904
~~Admiralty~~
M 0287

9. 7 / 3 / 04

~~to F. O.~~

ON HIS MAJESTY'S SERVICE.

4. m map book

ADMIRALTY

reply quote
M
fidential.

Admiralty,

12th January 1904.

Sir,	With reference to your letter of the 8th
instant, I am commanded by My Lords Commissioners

of the Admiralty to transmit for the information of the Secretary

of State for	Foreign Affairs, copy

of a telegram dated of this date No. 13 from the

Commander in Chief, China, in reply

to Admiralty telegram No. 17

I am, Sir,

Your obedient Servant,

Evan MacGregor

Under Secretary of State,
Foreign Office.

Telegram No. 13

From **Commander-in-Chief,**
     China

	Place	Day	Time
Despatch	Tsingy	12 Jan 04	
Receipt	Admiralty	do	

Your 17. Landing of British Legation Guard reported in my telegram No 9. At the same time "Cressy" S.N.O at Chemulpo received orders to be prepared to reinforce if requested by British Minister, and, in the event of "Cressy" being relieved, to direct relieving ship to be similarly prepared

Copy of Telegram No 17 to C-in-C China, dated 9th January 1904 :—

    Understand that detachment of 20 marines from "Sirius" has been sent to Seoul as guard for Legation. F.O. asks that arrangements should be made to reinforce the Guard on emergency arising

    Report what you are doing

Confidential.

Admiralty,

18ᵗʰ Janʸ 1904.

Sir,

I am commanded by My Lords Commissioners

of the Admiralty to transmit for the information of the Secretary

of State for Foreign Affairs, extract from

a telegram dated 18ᵗʰ inst No. 16 from the
Commander in Chief, China, relative
to the Legation Guards at Seoul.

I am, Sir,

Your obedient Servant,

Evan Macgregor

Telegram No. 16

From: bint China

	Place	Day	Time
Despatch	Hongkong	18 Jan. '04	
Receipt	Admiralty	~~~	

(Extract)

Thirty Russians proceeded to Seoul as Legation Guard on 12th Jan, 42 French on 16th Jan., 67 more U.S.A. Marines from Manila garrison on 15th Jan. British Minister Seoul is requesting Legation Guard be increased by 15 marines on 30th January. These will further reduce seagoing complements.

R: Jan 18, 1903

Seoul Legation Grand

trs. tel. giving details of further reinforcements by French & U.S. Govts.

Mr Gordan requests further reinforcement of 15 marines for January 30.

not printed

We have heard this from Mr Jordan who concurs in the necessity for the extra 15 men, and I solicited approval for landing them. The approval has been sent. L W

36 Corea

Telegram from Corean Minister for F.A.

Chefoo { D 11.55 am
{ R 9.47 am } Jan 21. 1904

"Vu les complications qui ont surgi entre la Russie et le Japon et vu les difficultés que semblent rencontrer les négociateurs à amener une solution pacifique, le gouvernement coréen par ordre de sa Majesté l'Empereur, déclare qu'il a pris la ferme résolution d'observer la plus stricte neutralité quel que soit le résultat des pourparlers actuellement engagés entre les dites Puissances.

1

I have received a letter from the Foreign Office dated 28th October 1903. to consider to settle the Corean difficulty between Japan and Russia, and I thoroughly understand that the British Government renders its efforts to preserve Corea as far as possible in accordance with the Anglo-Japanese Treaty and the said note.

But I beg to call attention again to the British Government that at present, the circumstances are developed very much, and if the Russo-Japanese war should come, the things would be much difficult after its conclusion; and therefore I ask the favour of the British Government to give fresh guarantee to preserve the Independence, sovereignty, integrity and privileges of Corea as they are now, on whichever side the victory may be decided.

The Corean Government, its people and myself shall be much appreciated if the British Government would so kind enough as to give a fresh note "quoting" the following

편저자　송재용宋宰鏞

대전 출생
단국대학교 문리과대학 국어국문학과 및 동 대학원 졸업(문학박사)
단국대학교 동양학연구소 연구원 · 연구교수 · 연구실장 역임.
비교민속학회 출판이사 및 일반이사, 동아시아고대학회 연구이사 역임.
현재 단국대학교 종합인력개발원 교수, 동아시아고대학회 총무이사,
　　　한국향토자 연구 전국협의회 산하 용산향토사학회 부회장.

■ 저서 및 논문
　저서:『우리 전통문화와의 만남』(한국문화사,2002) 외 20여권.
　논문:「미암일기 연구」,「여류문인 송덕봉의 생애와 문학」,「한국일기문학론 시고」,
　　　「권석주 연구」 등 50여편.

구한말 최초의 순국열사 이한응

초판 인쇄일　2007年 2月 15日
초판 발행일　2007年 3月 12日

편저자　송재용
발행처　제이앤씨　|　등록　제7-220호

132-040
서울시 도봉구 창동 624-1 현대홈시티 102-1206
전화 (02)992-3253(代)　|　팩스 (02)991-1285
홈페이지 www.jncbook.co.kr　|　전자우편 jncbook@hanmail.net

ISBN 978-89-5668-490-1　93900
정가 15,000원

이 책은 2003년도 정부(교육인적자원부)의 재원으로 한국학술진흥재단의
지원을 받아 수행된 연구과제임(KRF-2003-005-A00010)